SCOTTISH MUSEUMS
and
GALLERIES

THE GUIDE

front cover illustrations:

Osprey rising with prey. Part of the dramatic natural history display at Inverness Museum. [*Inverness Museum*]

The Achavrail Armlet, one of very few such Celtic pieces from the 1st–2nd century AD. Found in Sutherland earlier this century and now part of the collections at Inverness Museum. [*Inverness Museum*]

Lithograph of MacLeod of Lewis, probably by MacIan, from the collections of Museum nan Eilean, Stornoway. The MacLeods held the Island of Lewis from the 13th century until the early 17th century, when they were ousted by the MacKenzies of Kintail. [*Museum nan Eilean*]

back cover illustrations:

Morning in Glen Nevis by Arthur Perigal, from the collections of the Smith Art Gallery and Museum, Stirling. Recent conservation work on this painting was supported by a Glenfiddich Living Scotland Award. [*Smith Art Gallery and Museum*]

Burntisland Fair by Andrew Young. This 1910 painting has been used as the inspiration for Edwardian Fair displays at Burntisland Museum. [*Kirkcaldy Museums and Art Gallery*]

Pit head workings at Lady Victoria Colliery, Newtongrange, now the home of the Scottish Mining Museum. [*Scottish Mining Museum*]

SCOTTISH MUSEUMS
and
GALLERIES

THE GUIDE

ABERDEEN UNIVERSITY PRESS and
SCOTTISH MUSEUMS COUNCIL
in association with
THE SUNDAY MAIL

First published 1990
Aberdeen University Press
Member of Maxwell Macmillan Pergamon Publishing Corporation

© Scottish Museums Council 1990

British Library Cataloguing in Publication Data

Scottish museums & galleries, the guide
1. Scotland. Museums
I. Scottish Museums Council
069.09411

ISBN 0 08 037974 5

compiled by Wilma Alexander and Lesley Castell

The information quoted in this book is as supplied to the Scottish Museums Council and to the best of our knowledge was correct at the time of going to press. There may be subsequent amendments particularly to admission charges and opening times and the publishers can accept no responsibility for any errors or omissions.

Typeset from author generated discs
and printed by AUP Glasgow/Aberdeen—A member of BPCC Ltd

Foreword

The increase in both number and quality of Scotland's museums and galleries constitutes a major success story of recent years.

They now represent an important part of the educational and cultural life of our nation.

After looking at this guide, I think you will wish to build visits to museums into your plans for travelling within Scotland. This can become a rewarding habit.

I have pleasure in commending it to you.

Lord Balfour of Burleigh

Contents

Black and White Illustrations

Colour Plates

Pit head workings at Lady Victoria Colliery, Newtongrange, now the home of the Scottish Mining Museum. *frontispiece*

between pages 6 and 7

The library at Abbotsford, Melrose, home of Sir Walter Scott where many of his most famous novels were written.

Portrait of a Man in a Red Tunic by E A Hornel, in Broughton House, Kirkcudbright.

View of the harbour at Kirkcudbright, from the collections of Broughton House, Kirkcudbright.

between pages 22 and 23

Courtyard of the Scottish Fisheries Museum, Anstruther.

Jo Barker, Artist-in-Residence at Aberdeen Art Gallery in 1988, at work in the Studio Workshop.

Part of a display on the diversity of human cultures at the Marischal Museum, University of Aberdeen.

between pages 54 and 55

'An American Girl' by Gerald Laing, part of the permanent collection at Inverness Museum and Art Gallery.

Tam Docherty in his room at the Grove Street Model Lodging House, during the 1970s.

A friendly word from a warder in the Main Hall of the Royal Museum of Scotland, Edinburgh.

between pages 70 and 71

Inveraray Jail, the dramatically-situated 19th century prison which now houses a museum re-creating prison life.

The Denny Ship Model Experimental Tank.

'Princess Cecily', stained glass portrait on view at the Burrell Collection, Glasgow.

One of the spacious galleries at the Burrell Collection, Glasgow.

between pages 86 and 87

Kelvin Street with toy shop and fish shop, Museum of Transport.

Motor cycle display, Museum of Transport.

Reconstruction of the 'single end' where David Livingstone was born.

between pages 94 and 95

Mural commissioned by Dundee Museums and Art Galleries from local students.

Royal Research Ship *Discovery*, built in Dundee.

Blair Castle, Blair Atholl, home of the 10th Duke of Atholl.

Signpost to the Museum at Shawbost.

How to use this Guide

The entries in this guide are divided geographically into Scotland's Regions and Island Councils. For each region, a map shows the approximate location of sites. The entries are sorted alphabetically under the name of the town or nearest town and then listed by museum or gallery. The layout of each entry is shown below.

Opening times and details of facilities are correct at time of going to press but may be subject to change. Many museums close on public holidays, including local holidays, so visitors should check the local press for details.

An alphabetical index of museum/gallery names is given at the end of this guide.

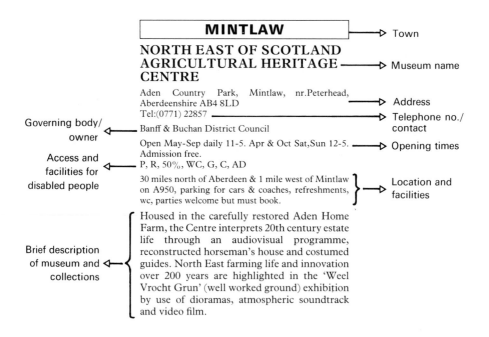

MINTLAW — ▷ Town

NORTH EAST OF SCOTLAND AGRICULTURAL HERITAGE — ▷ Museum name **CENTRE**

Aden Country Park, Mintlaw, nr.Peterhead, Aberdeenshire AB4 8LD — ▷ Address
Tel:(0771) 22857 — ▷ Telephone no./contact

Governing body/owner — Banff & Buchan District Council

Open May-Sep daily 11-5. Apr & Oct Sat,Sun 12-5. — ▷ Opening times
Admission free.

Access and facilities for disabled people — P, R, 50%, WC, G, C, AD

30 miles north of Aberdeen & 1 mile west of Mintlaw on A950, parking for cars & coaches, refreshments, wc, parties welcome but must book. — ▷ Location and facilities

Brief description of museum and collections — Housed in the carefully restored Aden Home Farm, the Centre interprets 20th century estate life through an audiovisual programme, reconstructed horseman's house and costumed guides. North East farming life and innovation over 200 years are highlighted in the 'Weel Vrocht Grun' (well worked ground) exhibition by use of dioramas, atmospheric soundtrack and video film.

Access and Facilities for Disabled Visitors

The abbreviations used for disabled access and facilities are given below. This system was compiled with help from the Scottish Council on Disability. Visitors with special requirements are advised to contact the museum or gallery before visiting. This information has been supplied by the museums and while every effort has been made to ensure it is correct, the publishers cannot accept responsibility for any errors which may appear.

Parking available for disabled drivers	P
Parking available if pre-arranged	PPA
Level access to building	L
Ramped access to building	R
Stepped access to building	ST
Approximate proportion of exhibition space accessible	
All	100%
Half	50%
Less than half	<50%
Adapted toilet	WC
Induction loop system for the hard of hearing	H
Guide dogs allowed	G
Catering facilities accessible	C
Bar accessible	B
Audio description available	AD
Sign language available	SL

Regions

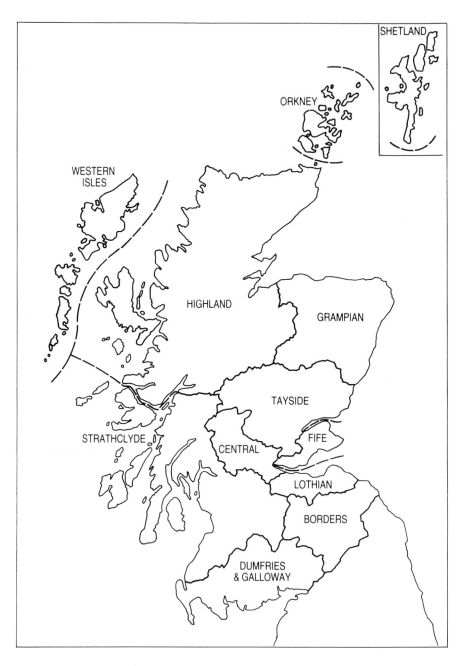

SHETLAND

ORKNEY

WESTERN
ISLES

HIGHLAND

GRAMPIAN

TAYSIDE

STRATHCLYDE

FIFE

CENTRAL

LOTHIAN

BORDERS

DUMFRIES
& GALLOWAY

Introduction

The Scottish Museums Council, which seeks to encourage and improve the work of museums throughout the country, has joined with Aberdeen University Press to produce this guide which should help you to plan your visits to Scotland's museums and galleries.

Since the Council began its work in 1964, the number, scope and quality of museums has increased and improved dramatically. Now we are looking forward to the 21st century, when barriers and divisions of all kinds between countries in Europe and elsewhere seem increasingly contrived. Whatever the politicians and power-wielders may effect, the institutions listed in this book will meanwhile show international visitors and Scots alike the story of the world from its origins and Scotland's place in it; the proof of how much Scots have gained from, shared with and given to other peoples in the wider world; an insight into the rise and fall, diminution and growth, of Scottish places and ways of life; and some hints at how to imagine everybody's futures. The wise visitor will also judge, and learn more from, the chronological evolution of technologies from hunting and pottery to mechanised agriculture and microchip-controlled production, and the overlapping developments at any time in history from the simplest traditional crafts to the most sophisticated or emotional works of individual art.

Our heritage (that much-abused word) is meaningless without awareness of where it began and where it still may lead. Our galleries and museums are by far the most pleasurable, painless and aggression-free places to make those discoveries. Make the most of them!

A Trevor Clark
CBE LVO MA FSAScot
Chairman, Scottish Museums Council

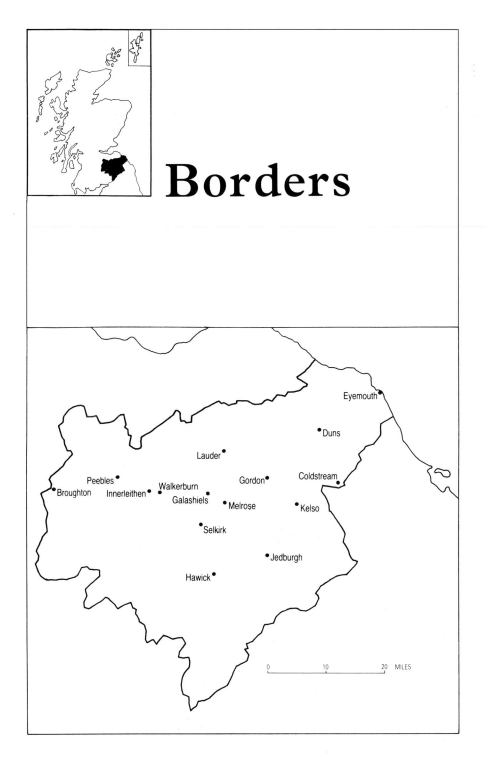

Borders

BROUGHTON

JOHN BUCHAN CENTRE

Broughton, Biggar ML12 6HQ
Tel:(0899) 21050

Biggar Museum Trust

Open Easter-mid Oct daily 2-5. Admission charges (with concessions).
P, R/ST, 100%, WC, G

On A701 (Edinburgh-Moffat Road), parking for cars & coaches, sales area, wc, parties welcome but must book.

The centre is dedicated to John Buchan, author of 'The Thirty Nine Steps', lawyer, politician, soldier, historian, biographer, poet and Governor General of Canada; a true Renaissance man.

COLDSTREAM

COLDSTREAM MUSEUM

Coldstream, Berwickshire
Tel:(0890) 2630
Correspondence to Museums Services Officer, Berwickshire District Council, 8 Newtown Street, Duns, Berwickshire TD11 3DU. Tel:(0361) 82600.

Coldstream Museum Committee

For opening times tel:(0890) 2360 or 2607. Admission charges.
ST, 50%, G

Market square, parking for cars & coaches, sales area, wc, parties welcome no need to book.

A local history museum which tells the story of Coldstream using items donated and loaned by local people. There is also a display of material belonging to the Coldstream Guards.

THE HIRSEL HOMESTEAD MUSEUM & CRAFT CENTRE

The Hirsel, Coldstream, Berwickshire TD12 4LP
Tel:(0890) 2834/2965

Douglas & Angus Estates

Open all year daily during reasonable daylight hours. Admission charges.
P, L, 100%, WC, G, C

1 mile from Coldstream, parking for cars & coaches, refreshments, sales area, wc, parties welcome no need to book (except for teas).

Housed in 19th century carriage houses and stables, the museum contains exhibits from all aspects of the estate's past, the evolution of the Hirsel and history of the Home family, including forestry, farming, archaeology and natural history. The craft workshops have exhibitions and demonstrations on most days. A study room may be booked. Nature walks and picnic area.

DUNS

JIM CLARK MEMORIAL ROOM

44 Newtown Street, Duns, Berwickshire
Tel:(0361) 82600
Correspondence to Museums Services Officer, Berwickshire District Council, 8 Newton Street, Duns, Berwickshire TD11 3DU. Tel:(0361) 82600.

Berwickshire District Council

Open Apr-Sep Mon-Sat 10-1 & 2-5 Sun 2-5. Admission charges.
P, ST, 100%

North of Berwick-on-Tweed on A6105 & A6112, parking for cars & coaches, parties welcome no need to book.

Trophies won by Jim Clark OBE, the former motor racing champion whose home town was Duns.

MANDERSTON

Duns, Berwickshire TD11 3PP
Tel:(0361) 83450

Mr. & Mrs. A. Palmer

Open mid May-Sep Thu & Sun 2-5.30. Other times by appointment. Admission charges (with concessions).
P, ST, 100%, G, C

1 1/2 miles south east of Duns on A6105, parking for cars & coaches, refreshments, sales area, temporary exhibitions, wc, parties welcome but must book.

Thought to be the finest Edwardian house in classical style in Britain, Manderston contains elegantly furnished rooms, a collection of samplers and many items made from Blue John (a semi-precious stone from Derbyshire). The house contains Britain's first private biscuit tin museum with many rare tins dating from 1873. Formal gardens and picturesque landscapes provide a unique setting.

EYEMOUTH

EYEMOUTH MUSEUM

Auldkirk, Market Place, Eyemouth, Berwickshire TD14 5HE
Tel:(08907) 50678

Eyemouth Museum Trust

Open Easter-Oct Mon-Sat 10-6 Sun 2-6. Admission charges (with concessions).

P, R, 50%, G, AD

Town centre, parking for cars & coaches, sales area, temporary exhibitions, parties welcome but must book.

This award-winning folk life and fishing museum was opened to commemorate the centenary of the great East Coast Fishing Disaster of 1881 when 189 local fishermen were drowned. This event is depicted in a 15ft tapestry which has received national acclaim.

GALASHIELS

GALASHIELS MUSEUM & EXHIBITION

Peter Anderson Ltd., Nether Mill, Huddersfield Street, Galashiels TD1 3BA
Tel:(0896) 2091

Peter Anderson Ltd.

Open Apr-Oct Mon-Thu 10.30-11.30 & 1.30-2.30, Fri 10.30-11.30. Admission to museum free, charge for factory tour.
P, L/R/ST, 100%, WC, G

Near town centre, parking for cars & coaches, sales area, temporary exhibitions, wc, parties welcome no need to book.

Opened in 1983 and situated in the Peter Anderson Mill Complex, this exhibition brings aspects of the town's past to life in a display of early photographs, artefacts of the woollen trade and domestic items. The refurbished Leffel water turbine wheel is harnessed to run a weaving loom within the museum. Conducted mill tours are available.

OLD GALA HOUSE

Scott Crescent, Galashiels TD1 3JS
Tel:(0896) 2611
Correspondence to District Curator, Ettrick & Lauderdale Museum Service, Municipal Buildings, High St, Selkirk TD7 4JX. Tel:(0750) 20096 or 20054.

Ettrick & Lauderdale District Council

Open Apr-Oct Mon-Sat 10-4 Sun 2-4. Other times by arrangement. Admission free.
PPA, R/ST, <50%, WC, G, C, AD

Town centre, parking for cars, refreshments, sales area, temporary exhibitions, wc, parties welcome.

Old Gala House, dating from 1583, was once the home of the Lairds of Gala. It re-opened as an interpretation centre in 1988. Displays tell the story of the House, the Lairds and the early development of Galashiels. Particularly memorable are the Painted Ceiling (1635) and the Painted Wall (1988). There is a display relating to Galashiels-born sculptor Thomas

Clapperton and two temporary exhibition galleries.

SCOTTISH COLLEGE OF TEXTILES

Netherdale, Galashiels TD1 3HF
Tel:(0896) 3351

Scottish Education Department

Open during term time Mon-Fri 9-5. Sat & Sun by appointment. Admission free.
PPA, R/ST, 100%, WC, G, C, AD, SL

1 1/2 miles out of town on south side, parking for cars & coaches, temporary exhibitions, wc, parties welcome but must book.

The college specialises in exhibitions catering for design students and supports the work of local artists.

GORDON

MELLERSTAIN HOUSE

Gordon, Berwickshire, TD3 6LG
Tel:(057 381) 225

Earl of Haddington

Open May-Sep Sun-Fri 12.30-5. Admission charges (with concessions).
P, ST, 50%, G, C

7 miles north west of Kelso on A6089, parking for cars & coaches, refreshments, sales area, temporary exhibitions, wc, parties welcome no need to book.

An extremely fine Adam house with beautiful period furniture. Fine art collection includes works by Gainsborough, Aikman, Allan Ramsay, Van Ruisdael and Van Dyck.

HAWICK

HAWICK MUSEUM & THE SCOTT GALLERY

Wilton Lodge Park, Hawick, Roxburghshire TD9 7JL
Tel:(0450) 73457

Roxburgh District Council

Open all year Apr-Sep Mon-Sat 10-12 & 1-5 Sun 2-5 Oct-Mar Mon-Fri 1-4 Sun 2-4. Admission charges (with concessions).
P, ST, G

1/2 mile west of town centre off A7, parking for cars, sales area, temporary exhibitions, wc, parties welcome but must book.

The museum and gallery stand in award-winning parkland, where a new garden for disabled visitors has just been completed. The museum has permanent displays which tell the story of the knitwear and hosiery industries of the area. Also natural history, domestic life, archaeological and geological exhibits are on display. The Scott Gallery, built in 1975, has a regular and varied temporary exhibition programme as well as its own collection of 19th and 20th century Scottish paintings.

INNERLEITHEN

ROBERT SMAIL'S PRINTING WORKS

High Street, Innerleithen, Peebles-shire
Tel:(0896) 830206

National Trust for Scotland

Printworks and shop open Jul-Oct Mon-Sat 10-1 & 2-5 Sun 2-5. Shop only May-Jul Mon, Wed-Sat 10-1 & 2-5. Admission free.
L, 50%, G

Town centre, parking nearby, sales area.

The building contains vintage working printing machinery, including a 100-year-old press which was originally driven by water-wheels. The Trust plans to re-open the printing works during 1990 as a time-capsule of yesteryear. The Victorian office of the printing firm, with original artefacts, is also on display.

TRAQUAIR HOUSE

Innerleithen, Peeblesshire EH44 6PW
Tel:(0896) 830 323

Private

Open daily Easter, late May-Sep 1.30-5.30 May only Sat-Sun 1.30-5.30 Jul-Aug also 10.30-5.30. Admission charges.
P, R/ST, G, C, B

Six miles east of Peebles on B709, parking for cars & coaches, refreshments, sales area, temporary exhibitions, wc, parties welcome no need to book.

The oldest inhabited house in Scotland, Traquair has sheltered 27 Scottish and English kings. Dating back to the 10th century it has associations with Mary Queen of Scots and the Jacobite risings. The 18th century library contains the original collection of books and family archives. A collection of treasures displayed throughout the house includes embroideries, glass, paintings, silver and porcelain. The 18th century brewhouse is still in full production and is licensed to sell its own beer. Licensed tearoom/restaurant, nature trails, maze, picnic area. Special events during season include pipe bands, music, exhibitions, antique fair and the Traquair Fair.

JEDBURGH

CASTLE JAIL

Castlegate, Jedburgh, Roxburghshire
Tel:(0835) 63254
Correspondence to Hawick Museum, Wilton Lodge Park, Hawick, Roxburghshire TD9 7LJ. Tel:(0450) 73457.

Roxburgh District Council

Open Easter-Sep daily 10-12 & 1-5 Sun 2-5. Admission charges (with concessions).
L, G

Up Castlegate from town centre, refreshments, sales area, wc, parties welcome but must book.

Built as a Howard reform prison in 1823, this building is the only existing example of its kind in Scotland. The museum has a small display of items relating to 19th century prison life.

MARY QUEEN OF SCOTS' HOUSE

Queen Street, Jedburgh, Roxburghshire TD8 6EN
Tel:(0835) 63331
Correspondence to Hawick Museum, Wilton Lodge Park, Hawick, Roxburghshire TD9 7LJ. Tel:(0450) 73457.

Roxburgh District Council

Open Easter-Oct daily 10-12 & 1-5 Sun 1-5. Admission charges (with concessions).
P, L, G

Town centre, parking nearby, sales area, wc, parties welcome but must book.

This fine example of a 16th century bastel house is set in public gardens. Exhibits relate to the Queen and her visit to Jedburgh in 1566.

KELSO

FLOORS CASTLE

Kelso, Roxburghshire
Tel:(0573) 23333

Duke of Roxburghe

Open Apr-Jun & Sep Sun-Thu Jul & Aug daily 10.30-4.45. Admission charges (with concessions).
P, L/ST, 100%, WC, G, C

3/4 mile north of Kelso on A6089, parking for cars & coaches, refreshments, sales area, wc, parties welcome but must book.

The home of the Roxburghe family was built in 1721 by William Adam with later additions by Playfair. Magnificent tapestries, fine French and English furniture, paintings and a large collection of porcelain are displayed in the castle. Walled garden, children's playground and licensed restaurant are amongst the other facilities.

KELSO MUSEUM

Turret House, Abbey Court, Kelso, Roxburghshire TD5 7JA
Tel:(0573) 25470
Correspondence to Hawick Museum, Wilton Lodge Park, Hawick, Roxburghshire TD9 7LJ. Tel:(0450) 73457.

Roxburgh District Council

Open Easter-Oct Mon-Sat 10-12 & 1-6 Sun 2-6. Admission charges (with concessions).
P, R, G

In Tourist Information Centre opposite Abbey, parking limited, sales area, parties welcome no need to book.

This museum shares a 17th century building, a property of the National Trust for Scotland, with the Tourist Information Centre. Displays interpret Kelso and its surroundings.

LAUDER

THIRLESTANE CASTLE

Lauder, Berwickshire TD2 6RU
Tel:(057 82) 430

Thirlestane Castle Trust

Open May,Jun,Sep Wed-Thu, Sun 2-5 Jul-Aug Sun-Fri 2-5. Admission charges (with concessions).
P, ST, 50%, WC, C

Parking for cars & coaches, refreshments, sales area, temporary exhibitions, wc, parties welcome but must book.

Historic castle and family home with superb 17th century ceilings. A large collection of historic toys are displayed in old family nurseries. Restored kitchens and laundries and exhibitions of rural life in the Scottish Borders over the centuries. Arrangements can be made for group visits out of season.

MELROSE

ABBOTSFORD HOUSE

Melrose, Roxburghshire TD6 9BQ
Tel:(0896) 2043

Mrs. P. Maxwell-Scott OBE

Open Mar-Oct Mon-Sat 10-5 Sun 2-5. Admission charges.
P, L/R, 100%, WC, G

3 1/2 miles from Melrose on B6360, parking for cars & coaches, refreshments, sales area, wc, parties welcome no need to book.

This 19th century mansion was built and occupied by Sir Walter Scott until his death. It contains the writer's extensive library (over 9,000 volumes) and a remarkable collection of relics associated with famous characters in Scotland's history, including Rob Roy's gun and Prince Charlie's quaich.

MELROSE ABBEY

Melrose, Roxburghshire
Tel:(031) 244 3101 for information.

Scottish Development Department (Historic Buildings and Monuments)

Open Oct-Mar Mon-Sat 9.30-4 Sun 2-4 Apr-Sep Mon-Sat 9.30-7 Sun 2-7. Admission charges (with concessions).
L/ST, G

A ruined, beautiful Cistercian abbey founded by David I but repeatedly wrecked by the English in the Wars of Independence. The Commendator's house contains material relating to the abbey's history and to the Roman fort at Newstead.

PEEBLES

THE CORNICE: SCOTTISH MUSEUM OF ORNAMENTAL PLASTERWORK

31 High Street, Peebles
Tel:(0721) 20212

L Grandison & Son

Open Apr-Jun & Sep Fri, Sun, Mon 2-4 Sat 10.30-12.30 & 2-4 Jul-Aug daily 2-4 and Fri-Mon also 10.30-12.30 Oct-Nov Sat, Sun only 2-4. Other times by arrangement. Admission charges (with concessions).

Town centre, parking nearby.

This museum recreates a plasterer's casting workshop of the late 19th-early 20th century, illustrating the methods of creating ornamental plasterwork using a collection of 'masters' from that time. This award-winning museum includes a 'hands-on' area for trying your own plastering - wellies and apron provided!

TWEEDDALE MUSEUM

Chambers Institute, High Street, Peebles EH45 8AP
Tel:(0721) 20123

Tweeddale District Council

Open all year Mon-Fri 10-1 & 2-5 Apr-Oct also Sat-Sun 2-5. Admission free.
L, ST, <50%, G

Town centre, temporary exhibitions, parties welcome but must book.

1 A reconstruction of an ironmongers' shop from the late 19th–early 20th century forms the centrepiece of Halliwell's House Museum in Selkirk. *[Antonia Reeve]*

The library at Abbotsford, Melrose, home of Sir Walter Scott where many of his most famous novels were written. [*Scottish Museums Council*]

View of the harbour at Kirkcudbright, from the collections of Broughton House, Kirkcudbright. [*E A Hornel's Trust*]

Broughton House, Kirkcudbright: *Portrait of a Man in a Red Tunic,* painted in 1884/5 by E A Hornel when he was a student in Antwerp. [*E A Hornel's Trust*]

Small local museum with changing displays relating to the history of the area. The Picture Gallery is used for a changing programme of contemporary art exhibitions.

SELKIRK

BOWHILL

Selkirk, TD7 5ET
Tel:(0750) 20732

Duke of Buccleuch & Queensberry KT

House open Jul Mon-Sat 1-4.30 Sun 2-6. Last admission 3/4 hour before closing. Country park open 28 Apr-28 Aug Mon-Thu & Sat 12-5 Sun 2-6. During Aug also Fri 12-5. Admission charges (with concessions).
P, R/ST, 100%, WC, G, C, B, AD, SL

3 miles west of Selkirk on A708, parking for cars & coaches, refreshments, sales area, temporary exhibitions, wc, parties welcome, booking preferred.

The historic house of Bowhill, dating from 1812, is still furnished with many of its original brocades and hand-painted Chinese wallpapers. Art treasures abound and there are interesting collections of personal relics belonging to the ancestors of the Duke of Buccleuch. A restored Victorian kitchen can also be seen. The house is open to schools and cultural parties by appointment between 1 May and 1 September. School packs and teachers' guides are available. There is an audio-visual presentation, lecture room and visitor centre. A picnic area and adventure playground are in the grounds.

HALLIWELL'S HOUSE MUSEUM

Halliwell's Close, Market Place, Selkirk TD7 4BL
Tel:(0750) 20096 or 20054
Correspondence to Museums Officer, Ettrick & Lauderdale District Council, Municipal Buildings, High Street, Selkirk TD7 4BU.

Ettrick & Lauderdale District Council

Open Apr-Oct Mon-Sat 10-5 Sun 2-4 Nov-Dec Mon-Fri 2-4.30 Sat-Sun 2-4. Admission charges (with concessions). Nov-Dec free.
L/R, <50%, WC, G, AD

Town centre, parking for cars & coaches, sales area, temporary exhibitions, wc, parties welcome but must book.

After extensive renovation, Selkirk's oldest dwelling house was opened in 1984 as a museum, sharing premises with the Tourist Information Centre. An extensive collection of ironmongery is displayed in a recreated ironmonger's shop. Other lively displays relate to the history of the building and to Selkirk. Temporary exhibitions are held in the Robson Gallery and video and audio-tape programmes are available.

WALKERBURN

SCOTTISH MUSEUM OF WOOLLEN TEXTILES

Tweedvale Mills, Walkerburn, Peeblesshire EH43 6AH
Tel:(089 687) 619

Tweedvale Mills

Open Easter-Oct Mon-Sat 9.30-5 Sun 11-5. Admission free.
P, L, G, C

Between Peebles & Galashiels on A72, parking for cars & coaches, refreshments, sales area, wc, parties welcome no need to book.

A fascinating history of the woollen industry from its origins as a cottage industry to the present day. An old weaver's cottage and shed, early wool patterns, cloth patterns and early tools are on display. Large mill shop and coffee shop.

2 Caledonian Railway locomotive No. 419, in steam at the Scottish Railway Preservation Society line at Bo'ness. *[D Bytheway]*

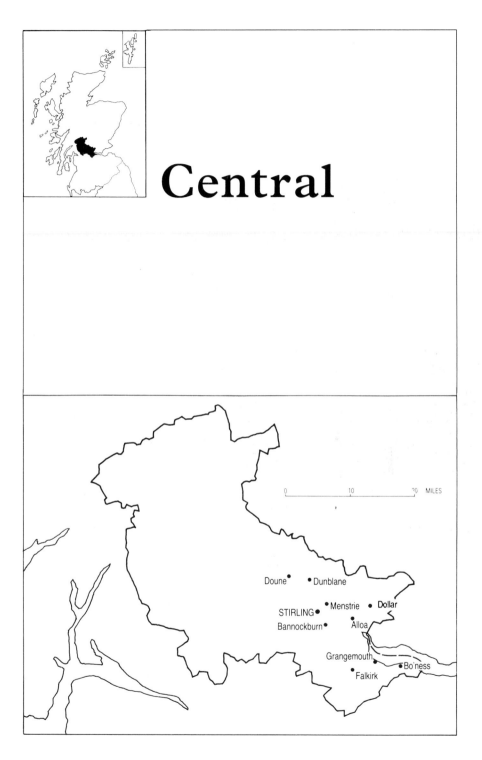

Central

Doune • • Dunblane

• Menstrie • Dollar
STIRLING •
Bannockburn • Alloa

Grangemouth •
• Falkirk • Bo'ness

0   10   20   MILES

ALLOA

ALLOA MUSEUM

Spiers Centre, Primrose Street, Alloa, Clackmannanshire FK10 1HT
Tel:(0259) 213131

Clackmannan District Council

Open all year Mon-Fri 10-4 Sat 10-12.30. Admission free.
PPA, R/ST, 100%, WC, G

Town centre, temporary exhibitions, parties welcome no need to book.

Small museum of mainly local interest. Touring exhibitions occasionally.

BO'NESS

BO'NESS & KINNEIL RAILWAY

The Station, Union Street, Bo'ness, West Lothian EH51 0AD
Tel:(0506) 822298

Scottish Railway Preservation Society

Steam trains run from Easter weekend to September 30, Sat & Sun & holiday Mon from 12-4.30, also Jul 14-Aug 19 Tue-Fri. Santa season in December. Admission to site free, charges for train fares (with concessions).
P, R, G

On the foreshore, parking for cars & coaches, refreshments, sales area, wc, parties welcome booking preferred.

The steam railway centre illustrates the history of the Scottish railways and of the companies operating before nationalisation. A working steam line with historic locomotives and rolling stock runs to Birkhill, where visitors can see the Birkhill Clay Mine. Track has been extended to a round trip of 3 miles from Bo'ness station to Kinneil. Special schools fortnight every year about May, special events some weekends.

BO'NESS HERITAGE AREA

Bo'ness Station, Bo'ness, West Lothian EH51 0AD
Tel:(0506) 825855

Bo'ness Heritage Trust

Foreshore sites open at all reasonable times. Admission free but charge for Birkhill Clay Mine.

Signposted Heritage Museum from Bo'ness, parking for cars & coaches, wc, parties welcome but must book.

A number of integrated sites are being developed in the Heritage area, including reconstructed buildings, maritime exhibits and an underground experience at Birkhill Clay Mine. Trails, guided walks and events help unlock the story of Scotland's industrial heritage and of Bo'ness itself. The sites are linked by steam-operated Bo'ness and Kinneil Railway.

KINNEIL MUSEUM & ROMAN FORTLET

Duchess Anne Cottages, Kinneil Estate, Bo'ness, West Lothian
Tel:(0506) 824318
Correspondence to Falkirk Museums Administration, Public Library, Hope Street, Falkirk FK1 5AU. Tel:(0324) 24911.

Falkirk District Council

Open Apr-Sep Mon-Fri 10-12.30 & 1.30-5 Sat 10-5 Jun-Aug also Sun 10-5 Oct-Mar Sat only 10-5. Admission free.
P, ST, 50%, G

Parking for cars, sales area, temporary exhibitions, wc, parties welcome but must book.

The museum is housed in the renovated stable block of Kinneil House. Displays on the lower floor deal with aspects of Bo'ness history, in particular pottery. On the upper floor an exhibition traces 2,000 years of history of the estate from Roman times to the present. Historical figures associated with the site include the Emperor Antoninus Pius, St Serf, Mary, Queen of Scots, and James Watt. An excavated Roman Fortlet can be seen a short walk from the museum. Guided tours of the estate are available in summer.

DOLLAR

DOLLAR MUSEUM

Old Schoolhouse, East Burnside, Dollar
Correspondence to Mrs Carolan, Hon. Curator, 55 Princes Crescent, Dollar. Tel:(0259) 42895.

Dollar Museum Trust

Open Feb-Nov Sat 10-12 Sun 2-4. Other times by appointment. Admission free.
P, ST, G

Town centre, parking for cars & coaches.

This small local history museum includes a display of the Provost's Regalia and photographs of Dollar in times gone by.

3   Visitors commencing a tour of Birkhill Clay Mine at Bo'ness. *[Scottish Museums Council]*

4   A school party engrossed in the displays at Kinneil Museum. *[Scottish Museums Council]*

DOUNE

DOUNE MOTOR MUSEUM

Doune, Perthshire FK16 6HD
Tel:(0786) 841203

Earl of Moray

Open Apr-Oct daily 10-5. Admission charges (with concessions).
P, L, 100%, G, C

8 miles north west of Stirling on A84, parking for cars & coaches, refreshments, sales area, wc, parties welcome no need to book.

A fine collection of vintage and classic motor cars. Over 40 cars on display, including a 1905 Rolls Royce, the second oldest in existence. Phone for details of motoring events held throughout the season.

DUNBLANE

DUNBLANE CATHEDRAL MUSEUM

The Cross, Dunblane, Perthshire
Tel:(0786) 824254
Correspondence to Curator, Mr John G Lindsay, The Square, Dunblane FK15 0AQ.

Society of Friends of Dunblane Cathedral

Open Easter, Jun-Sep Mon-Sat 10.30-12.30 & 2.30-4.30. Admission free.
P, L, 50%, G

North side of cathedral, parking nearby, sales area, parties welcome no need to book.

A miscellany of items relevant to the history of Dunblane and in particular the cathedral are displayed in the dean's house built in 1624.

FALKIRK

FALKIRK MUSEUM

15 Orchard Street, Falkirk FK1 1RF
Correspondence to Falkirk District Administration, Public Library, Hope Street, Falkirk FK1 5AU. Tel:(0324) 24911.

Falkirk District Council

Open all year Mon-Sat 10-12.30 & 1.30-5. Admission free.
ST, G

200 yards from both bus & rail stations, sales area, temporary exhibitions, parties welcome but must book.

The district's principal museum has displays tracing the history and development of the area from the earliest times. Displays include Roman and Medieval pottery, Dunmore pottery, locally produced cast-iron objects and photographs and archives relating to industrial and rural life.

GRANGEMOUTH

GRANGEMOUTH MUSEUM

Public Library, Bo'ness Road, Grangemouth, Stirlingshire
Correspondence to Falkirk Museums Administration, Public Library, Hope Street, Falkirk FK1 5AU. Tel:(0324) 24911.

Falkirk District Council

Open all year Mon-Sat 2-5. Admission free.

Sales area, parties welcome but must book.

This recently refurbished museum tells the story of one of Scotland's earliest planned industrial towns, from its origins as the East terminus of the Forth and Clyde canal to its present status as a major centre for the petroleum and chemical industries.

MUSEUM WORKSHOP

7-11 Abbotsinch Road, Abbotsinch Industrial Estate, Grangemouth
Tel:(0324) 471853
Correspondence to: Falkirk Museums Administration, Public Library, Hope Street, Falkirk FK1 5AU. Tel:(0324) 24911.

Falkirk District Council

Open Jul-Aug Mon-Fri 10-5 and 'Open Weeks' regularly throughout the year, see Press or Museum Service information. Admission free.
P, ST, 50%, G

Parking for cars, sales area.

These premises are the main store for Falkirk District Museums Service and a workshop for projects such as the restoration of a 1931 Falkirk tram and the building of a replica of the 'Charlotte Dundas', the world's first practical steamship.

MENSTRIE

MENSTRIE CASTLE

Castle Road, off Brook Street, Menstrie, Clackmannanshire
Contact NTS Regional Office. Tel:(0738) 31296.

National Trust for Scotland / Clackmannan District Council

Open by arrangement. Admission charges.
ST, G

5 miles north east of Stirling off A91, parking nearby, parties welcome no need to book.

A 16th century castle now converted to modern use where a commemoration room tells the story of the Nova Scotia Baronetcies and displays the coats-of-arms of 109 existing baronets. Also contains a display on Sir William Alexander (1567-1640).

RUSKIE

RUSKIE FARM & LANDSCAPE MUSEUM

Dunaverig, Ruskie, Thornhill, by Stirling FK8 3QW
Tel:(078 685) 277

Lewis & Sarah Stewart

Open by appointment, book with farm or Stirling Tourist Office. Admission charges.
P, G

Off A84 west of Thornhill, parking for cars & coaches, refreshments, sales area, temporary exhibitions, wc, parties welcome but must book.

Sited on a working farm, this museum features exhibits from the old parish of Ruskie and its agricultural development over the centuries. Lively displays of models, photographs, implements etc. are housed in original farm buildings. Drystane dykes and the history of land ownership are just two of the many subjects covered.

STIRLING

THE ARGYLL & SUTHERLAND HIGHLANDERS REGIMENTAL MUSEUM

The Castle, Stirling FK8 1EH
Tel:(0786) 75165

The Argyll & Sutherland Highlanders

Open Easter-Sep Mon-Sat 10-6 Sun 11-5.30 Oct Mon-Fri 10-4. Admission free but admission charge to Stirling Castle.

Castle esplanade, parking for cars & coaches, refreshments, sales area, wc, parties welcome no need to book.

This museum portrays the history of the Regiment from 1794 to the present day through displays including uniforms, weapons, pictures, colours, medals and other militaria. There are dioramas and an audio-visual commentary.

BANNOCKBURN HERITAGE CENTRE

Bannockburn, Stirling FK7 0LJ
Tel:(0786) 812664

National Trust for Scotland

Site open all year, exhibition Apr-Oct daily 10-6. Admission charges (with concessions).
P, L, 100%, WC, H, G, AD

2 miles south of Stirling off M80/M9 at junction 9, parking for cars & coaches, sales area, wc, parties welcome but must book.

On the battlefield nearby, in June 1314, King Robert the Bruce routed the forces of King Edward II to win freedom for the Scots from English domination. This centre displays an exhibition telling the story as well as providing tourist information facilities.

MACROBERT ARTS CENTRE GALLERY

University of Stirling, Stirling FK9 4LA
Tel:(0786) 73171 ext. 2549

University of Stirling

Open Feb-May & Sep-Dec Tue-Sat 11-5 Sun 2-5 also 30 minutes before theatre performances & during intervals. Admission free.
P, L, 100%, WC, H, G, C, B, SL

3 miles north west of Stirling off A9, parking for cars & coaches, refreshments, sales area, temporary exhibitions, wc, parties welcome but must book.

An extremely varied programme of temporary exhibitions within a university arts complex. The theatre is used all year round for films, music, dance, theatre, conferences and children's shows.

SMITH ART GALLERY & MUSEUM

40 Albert Place, Dumbarton Road, Stirling
Tel:(0786) 71917

Stirling Smith Art Gallery & Museum Joint Committee

Open all year Apr-Sep Tue-Sat 10.30-5 Sun 2-5 Oct-Mar Tue-Fri 12-5 Sat 10.30-5 Sun 2-5. Admission free.
P, R/ST, 100%, WC, G, C

Town centre, parking for cars & coaches, refreshments, sales area, temporary exhibitions, wc, parties welcome no need to book.

Stirling's local history museum features the story of Stirling from William Wallace to the present day. Exhibitions programme includes selections from the museum's own excellent regional collections as well as contemporary arts and crafts touring exhibitions.

5   The Robert Burns Centre, housed in the old Town Mill (1781) on the banks of the River Nith, Dumfries. *[Nithsdale District Council Museums]*

Dumfries and Galloway

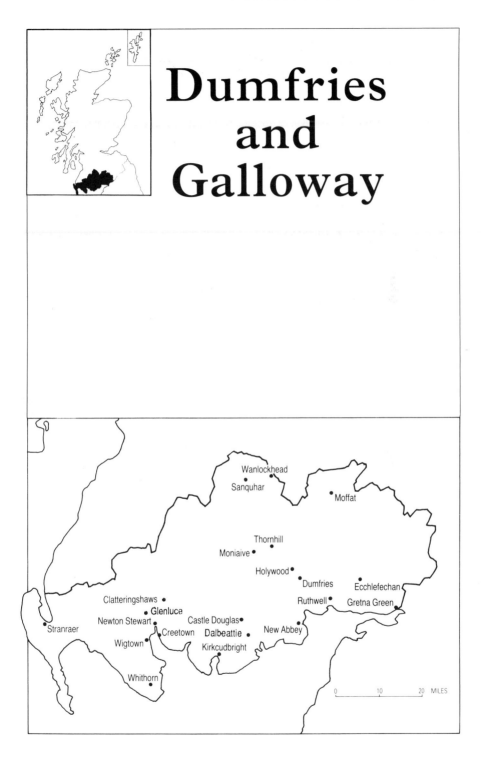

CASTLE DOUGLAS

CASTLE DOUGLAS ART GALLERY

Market Street, Castle Douglas DG7 1BE
Tel:(0557) 30291
Correspondence to Director of Administration, Council Offices, Kirkcudbright DG6 4JG.

Stewartry District Council

Gallery locked - key can be obtained during office hours from District Council Offices, St. Andrew Street, Castle Douglas. Admission free.
P, ST, 100%, G

Town centre, parking for cars & coaches, temporary exhibitions, wc, parties welcome but must book.

Stewartry District Council's art gallery houses a permanent collection of paintings by Mrs. Ethel S.G. Bristowe and has a programme of temporary exhibitions of mostly local artists.

CLATTERINGSHAWS

GALLOWAY DEER MUSEUM

Clatteringshaws, Kirkcudbrightshire
Tel:(06442) 285

Forestry Commission

Open Apr-Sep daily 10-5. Admission free.
P, R, 100%, WC, G, C

6 miles west of New Galloway by Clatteringshaws Loch on A712, parking for cars & coaches, wc, parties welcome no need to book.

This small museum tells the story of the red deer in Galloway. Galloway's wild goats and other local natural history are also illustrated.

CREETOWN

CREETOWN GEM-ROCK MUSEUM

Chain Road, Creetown, Kirkcudbrightshire
Tel:(0671 82) 357

Stephenson Family

Open summer daily 9.30-6, winter daily 9.30-5 Jan-Feb by appointment. Admission charges (with concessions).
P, L, 100%, G, C

Off A75, parking for cars & coaches, refreshments, sales area, temporary exhibitions, wc, parties welcome but must book.

The museum is a treasure house of fine mineral and gemstone specimens from around the world. Displays include special collections of dazzling fluorescent minerals, cut gemstones, fossils and mining equipment. There is a

Scottish agate collection and samples of Wanlockhead minerals. The lapidary workshop is open to the public.

DALBEATTIE

DALBEATTIE MUSEUM

Southwick Road, Dalbeattie, Kirkcudbrightshire
Correspondence to Mr D T Henderson, 231 High St, Dalbeattie, Kirkcudbrightshire. Tel:(0556) 610437.

Dalbeattie Museum Trust

Opening times to be arranged. Admission charges.
PPA, L, 50%, G

Town centre, parking nearby, sales area, wc.

This new museum will be partially open from Easter 1990. It will include displays on the local granite quarrying industry, shipping, the railway, and the history of the many mills which once operated at the Barr Burn.

DUMFRIES

BURNS' HOUSE

Burns Street, Dumfries DG1 2PS
Tel:(0387) 55297
Correspondence to Curator, Dumfries Museum, The Observatory, Church Street, Dumfries. Tel:(0387) 53374.

Nithsdale District Council

Open all year Apr-Sep Mon-Sat 10-1 & 2-5 Sun 2-5 Oct-Mar Tue-Sat 10-1 & 2-5. Admission charges (with concessions).
ST, 50%, G

1/4 mile from town centre, parking for cars & coaches, sales area, parties welcome but must book.

Robert Burns died in this house, his home during the last years of his life. Furnishings are of the period and many relics of the poet are on display.

DUMFRIES MUSEUM & CAMERA OBSCURA

The Observatory, Dumfries DG2 7SW
Tel:(0387) 53374

Nithsdale District Council

Open all year Apr-Sep Mon-Sat 10-1 & 2-5 Sun 2-5 Oct-Mar Tue-Sat 10-1 & 2-5. Admission to museum free, charges Apr-Sep for Camera Obscura.
P, R, 50%, WC, G

1/2 mile from Dumfries town centre on west of river, parking nearby, sales area, temporary exhibitions, wc, parties welcome no need to book.

Founded in 1835 as an astronomical observatory and museum, displays include fossil footprints left by prehistoric animals, a large collection of Nithsdale's minerals, birds of the Solway salt marshes, prehistoric tools and weapons, and early Christian carved stones. There are also sections on the history of the Royal Burgh of Dumfries and everyday Victorian working and home life.

GRACEFIELD ARTS CENTRE

28 Edinburgh Road, Dumfries DG1 1JQ
Tel:(0387) 63822

Dumfries & Galloway Regional Council Education Dept.

Open all year Apr-Sep Tue-Sat 10-5 Sun 11-1 & 2-5 Oct-Mar Mon-Fri 12-5 Sat 10-5 Sun 11-1 & 2-5. Admission free.
P, L/R, 50%, WC, G, C, B

Near town centre beside River Nith, parking for cars & coaches, cafe, temporary exhibitions, wc, parties welcome but must book.

The gallery contains a collection of important paintings by 19th and 20th century Scottish artists (the Faeds, Hornel, Jessie M. King, Elizabeth Blackadder, Alan Davie to name a few) and also has a varied exhibition programme of contemporary works by local and national artists. The Studios building houses an exhibition hall and workshop/studios, and the grounds contain a sculpture garden.

OLD BRIDGE HOUSE

Mill Road, Dumfries DG2 7BQ
Tel:(0387) 56904
Correspondence to Curator, Dumfries Museum, The Observatory, Church Street, Dumfries DG2 7SW.
Tel:(0387) 53374.

Nithsdale District Council

Open Apr-Sep Mon-Sat 10-1 & 2-5 Sun 2-5. Admission free.
P, ST, <50%, G

On Dumfries Old Bridge, parking nearby, sales area, parties welcome but must book.

The interesting period rooms in this 17th century house include kitchens c.1850 and 1900, a Victorian nursery and a dental laboratory dating from 1900.

ROBERT BURNS CENTRE

Old Town Mill, Mill Road, Dumfries DG2 7BE
Tel:(0387) 64808
Correspondence to Curator, Dumfries Museum, The Observatory, Church Street, Dumfries DG2 7SW.
Tel:(0387) 53374.

Nithsdale District Council

Open all year Apr-Sep Mon-Sat 10-8 Sun 2-5 Oct-Mar Tue-Sat 10-1 & 2-5. Admission free but charge for audiovisual programme.
P, R/ST, 100%, WC, H, G, C, B

1/3 mile from Dumfries town centre, on west bank of river, parking for cars & coaches, refreshments, sales area, wc, parties welcome no need to book.

Burns interpretation centre containing audio-visual programme and exhibition on Burns and his life in Dumfries.

ECCLEFECHAN

CARLYLE'S BIRTHPLACE

Ecclefechan, Dumfriesshire DG11 3DG
Tel:(057 63) 666

National Trust for Scotland

Open Apr-Oct Mon-Sat 12-5. Admission charges (with concessions).
ST, G

5 1/2 miles south east of Lockerbie off A74, parking nearby, parties welcome but must book.

Thomas Carlyle (1795-1881) writer and historian was born in this house. It is furnished appropriately and contains manuscripts and mementoes connected with his life and work.

GLENLUCE

GLENLUCE MOTOR MUSEUM

Glenluce, Newton Stewart, Wigtownshire
Tel:(05813) 534

Private

Open Mar-Oct daily 10-7 Nov-Feb Wed-Fri 11-4. Admission charges.
P, L, 100%, WC, G, C

At Glenluce on A75, parking for cars, refreshments, sales area, wc.

A collection of cars and motorbikes with motoring memorabilia including petrol cans and pumps, lights, and model cars.

GRETNA GREEN

FAMOUS OLD BLACKSMITH'S SHOP

Gretna Green, Dumfriesshire
Tel:(0461) 224

Gretna Museum & Tourist Services Ltd.

Open all year Mar-Oct daily 9-8, reduced hours in winter. Admission charges.
P, R, 100%, WC, G, C, B

Gretna 1/2 mile off A74, parking for cars & coaches, refreshments, sales area, wc, parties welcome no need to book.

Reminders of the days when young English couples eloped across the Border, taking advantage of Scotland's marriage laws. Marriage anvil, relics of the past and a collection of coaches on display.

HOLYWOOD

ELLISLAND FARM

Holywood, Dumfriesshire DG2 0RP
Tel:(038 774) 426
Correspondence to Hon. Secretary J.H. Dickie, Municipal Chambers, Buccleuch Street, Dumfries DG1 2AD.

The Ellisland Trust

Open at all reasonable times. Admission free.
ST, G

Approx 6 miles from Dumfries on A76, parking for cars, coaches in access road, parties welcome no need to book.

The farmhouse built by Burns in 1785 is lived in by resident curators. In Burns' old parlour there is a collection of exhibits connected with the poet and his family including his seal, letters, books, travelling-case (made from a tree-trunk) and the official tools (sword and scales) of his job as an exciseman. The adjoining granary has an exhibition of agricultural methods and implements. The grounds are associated with several of Burns' poems and songs including 'Tam O'Shanter', 'Auld Lang Syne' and 'Scots Wha Ha'e'.

KIRKCUDBRIGHT

BROUGHTON HOUSE

High Street, Kirkcudbright
Tel:(0557) 30437

E.A. Hornel's Trust

Open Easter-mid Oct Wed-Mon 11-1 & 2-5 Sun 2-5. Admission charges.
ST, 50%, G

Town centre, parking for cars & coaches, sales area, temporary exhibitions, parties welcome but must book.

The house and garden where artist E A Hornel (1864-1933) lived. The gallery contains a permanent exhibition of Hornel's pictures. The antiquarian library houses publications associated with the south west of Scotland, along with important manuscripts connected with Robert Burns.

STEWARTRY MUSEUM

St. Mary Street, Kirkcudbright
Tel:(0557) 31643

Stewartry Museum Association

Open Easter-Oct Mon-Sat 11-4 Jul-Aug 11-5. Admission charges.
P, ST, 50%, G

Town centre, parking for cars & coaches, temporary exhibitions, wc, parties welcome but must book.

Pomanders, pistols and poaching deterrents are just some of the items housed in this local museum, purpose-built in 1891. Collections of firearms, tools, agricultural implements, uniforms and lace as well as exhibits from prehistory, natural history and shipping can be seen under one roof. Delightful bookjackets and illustrations by the artist Jessie M. King (1875-1949) and sketches by her husband E.A. Taylor are some of the works by local artists on display.

MOFFAT

MOFFAT MUSEUM

The Neuk, Church Gate, Moffat DG10 9EG
Tel:(0683) 20868

Moffat Museum Trust

Open Easter, end May-Sep Mon,Tue,Thu-Sat 10.30-1 & 2.30-5 Sun 2.30-5. Admission charges.
P, ST, <50%

Centre of Moffat off A74 on A701, temporary exhibitions, parties welcome but must book.

Housed in an old bakery (the oven c.1850 was used until recently) the museum tells the story of the rise of Moffat as a Victorian spa town. Sporting pastimes, religious life, education and famous people associated with Moffat are just some of the topics covered. Small temporary exhibitions change frequently.

MONIAIVE

MAXWELTON MUSEUM

Maxwelton House, Moniaive, by Thornhill, Dumfriesshire DG3 4DX
Tel:(084 82) 385

Maxwelton House Trust

Open Jul & Aug Wed-Sun 2-5. Admission charges.
P, L, WC, G

13 miles north west of Dumfries on B729 near Moniaive, parking for cars & coaches, wc, parties welcome no need to book.

Dating from the 14th/15th centuries, this house was originally a stronghold of the Earls of Glencairn and later the birth-place of Annie Laurie to whom William Douglas of Fingland wrote the famous poem 'Maxwelton Braes are Bonny'. Admission covers the museum of early kitchen, dairy and small farming implements, private chapel, Annie Laurie's boudoir and gardens.

NEW ABBEY
SHAMBELLIE HOUSE MUSEUM OF COSTUME
New Abbey, Dumfriesshire
Tel: (038 785) 375
Correspondence to Royal Museum of Scotland, Chambers Street, Edinburgh EH1 1JF. Tel:(031) 225 7534.

Trustees of the National Museums of Scotland

Open May-Sep Thu-Mon 10-5.30 Sun 12-5.30. Admission free.
PPA, ST, 50%

7 miles from Dumfries on the A710, parking for cars, sales area, temporary exhibitions, wc, parties welcome but must book.

Each year this museum exhibits a new display of European fashionable dress from the National Costume collection.

NEWTON STEWART
THE MUSEUM
York Road, Newton Stewart, Wigtownshire
Correspondence to Miss H. Drew, Corsbie Cottage, Newton Stewart, Wigtownshire DG8 6JB.

Newton Stewart Civic Amenities Association

Open Easter week, May-Sep Mon-Sat 2-5 Jul-Sep also Sun 2-5, Jul-Aug also Sun 10-12.30. Admission charges.
P, L/R, G

Town centre, parking for cars & coaches, sales area, temporary exhibitions, parties welcome but must book.

This local museum describes the domestic and agricultural life of the area and contains displays of costume, white work lace, toys, tools, kitchen utensils and agricultural machinery. The museum also features a Victorian nursery and local photographs from the past.

RUTHWELL
SAVINGS BANK MUSEUM
Ruthwell, Dumfriesshire DG1 4NN
Tel:(038 787) 640

TSB Group, plc.

Open all year daily summer 10-1 & 2-5 winter Tue-Sat only. Admission free.
P, L, 100%, WC, G, AD

10 miles south of Dumfries off B724, parking for cars, coaches must book, sales area, temporary exhibitions, wc, parties welcome but must book.

This museum celebrates the life and work of the Rev. Henry Duncan D.D. (1774-1846) in the room where he founded the first savings bank in 1810. Original documents trace the growth of the worldwide savings bank movement from its Scottish beginnings. In addition to displays on the social history of the 19th century Scottish village, Dr Duncan's restoration of Ruthwell's 7th century Runic cross is documented.

SANQUHAR
SANQUHAR MUSEUM
The Old Tolbooth, Sanquhar DG4 6BL
Tel:(0659) 50186
Correspondence to Curator, Dumfries Museum, The Observatory, Church Street, Dumfries. Tel:(0387) 53374.

Nithsdale District Council

Open Apr-Sep Tue-Sun 10-1 & 2-5. Admission free.
P, ST, 100%, G

Town centre, parking nearby, parties welcome but must book.

A small local history museum housed in the old tolbooth, built in 1735 by William Adam.

STRANRAER
CASTLE OF ST JOHN
Stranraer
Tel:(0776) 5088
Correspondence to: Stranraer Museum, The Old Town Hall, George Street, Stranraer

Wigtown District Museum Service

Apr-Sep Mon-Sat 10-5. Admission free.
ST, <50%, G, AD

Town centre, parking, sales area.

Exhibitions tell the history of the castle from its building in the medieval period to the Covenanters in the 17th Century and use as a town jail in the 18th and 19th centuries.

STRANRAER MUSEUM

The Old Town Hall, George Street, Stranraer
Tel:(0776) 5088

Wigtown District Museum Service

Open all year Mon-Sat 10-5. Admission free.
L, 100%, WC, G, AD

Town centre, parking nearby, sales area, temporary exhibitions, parties welcome no need to book.

Headquarters of the Wigtown District Museum Service, this museum has a temporary exhibition policy covering both local and national topics. Permanent displays deal with archaeology, farming and the Polar explorers John & James Ross.

THORNHILL

THE ALEX BROWN CYCLE COLLECTION

Drumlanrig Castle, Thornhill, Dumfriesshire DG3 4AQ
Tel:(0848) 31555
Correspondence to Alex Brown, 'Newbarn', Stenton, East Lothian EH42 1TB. Tel:(036 85) 226.

Scottish Cycle Museums Trust

Open May-Sep daily 11-5. Admission free.

3 miles north of Thornhill off A76, parking for cars & coaches, refreshments, sales area, wc.

A new museum devoted to the history of cycles and cycling, housed in part of historic Drumlanrig Castle.

DRUMLANRIG CASTLE

Thornhill, Dumfriesshire DG3 4AQ
Tel:(0848) 30248

Duke of Buccleuch & Queensberry KT

Open May-late Aug Fri-Wed times subject to change.
Admission charges (with concessions).
P, L/R, 100%, C

3 miles north of Thornhill off A76, parking for cars & coaches, refreshments, sales area, wc, parties welcome but must book.

The Dumfriesshire home of the Duke of Buccleuch and Queensberry K.T. was built in 1679 by his Douglas ancestors and contains a large collection of paintings including works by Holbein, Reynolds, Rembrandt and Ramsay, 18th century French furniture and Bonnie Prince Charlie relics. An important Roman fort was discovered nearby in 1984. The grounds contain formal gardens, woodland walks, an adventure play area and picnic area. There is also a centre for craftsmen in the old stable yard. Pre-booked school parties welcome for nature trail and castle projects.

WANLOCKHEAD

MUSEUM OF SCOTTISH LEAD MINING

Goldscaur Row, Wanlockhead, Dumfriesshire
Tel:(0659) 74387

Wanlockhead Museum Trust

Open Easter-Oct daily 11-4. Admission charges (with concessions).
P, L/R, 100%, WC, G

Via A74 & B797 or A76 & B797, parking for cars & coaches, sales area, temporary exhibitions, wc, parties welcome but must book.

This unique site museum illustrates the story of Scottish lead mining. One and a half miles of walkway past mine heads, pumping engines, ore processing and smelting sites make up the outdoor museum. The indoor museum exhibits relics from 250 years of lead mining.

WHITHORN

WHITHORN PRIORY

Whithorn, Wigtownshire
Tel:(031) 244 3101 for information.

Scottish Development Department (Historic Buildings and Monuments)

Open Oct-Mar Mon-Sat 9.30-4 Sun 2-4 Apr-Sep Mon-Sat 9.30-7 Sun 2-7. Admission charges (with concessions).
ST, G

In town.

The first Christian church in Scotland was founded on this site by St. Ninian in the early 5th century. The ruins of the 12th century church still stand. The small museum contains a group of fine early Christian stones, including the Monreith Cross.

WIGTOWN

WIGTOWN MUSEUM

Town Hall, Wigtown
Correspondence to Stranraer Museum, The Old Town Hall, George Street, Stranraer. Tel:(0776) 5088.

Wigtown District Museum Service

Open Jun-Aug Mon-Fri 2-4. Admission free.
P, 100%, G

Town centre, parking for cars & coaches, sales area, parties welcome but must book.

This museum has displays on the Wigtown Martyrs and other local material such as the Oddfellows and Louis McGuffie V.C. The museum includes a local archive and photographs.

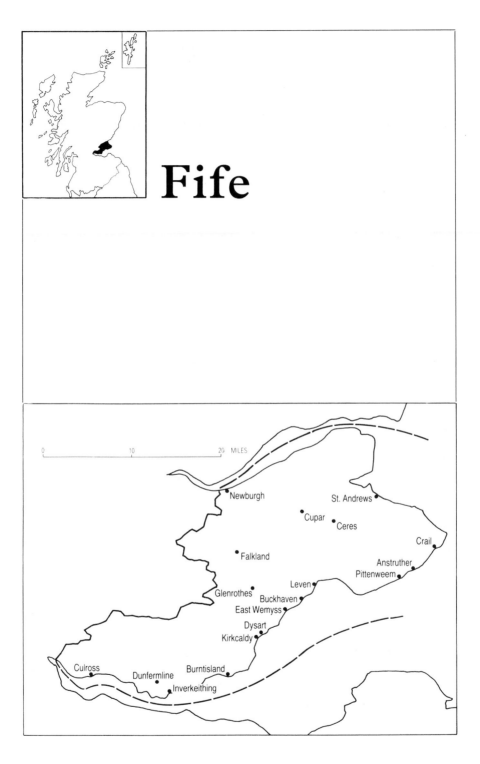

Fife

ANSTRUTHER

NORTH CARR LIGHT VESSEL

The Harbour, Anstruther, Fife
Tel:(0334) 53722
Correspondence to Curator, North East Fife District Council Dept. of Recreation, County Buildings, Cupar, Fife KY15 4TA. Tel:(0334) 53722.

North East Fife District Council

Open Apr-mid Oct daily 10-6. Admission charges.
P, R/ST, <50%, G, AD

Moored at the East Pier, parties welcome but must book.

A site museum with a difference. The North Carr was the last manned light vessel in service, on station from 1933-1974.

SCOTTISH FISHERIES MUSEUM

Harbourhead, Anstruther, Fife KY10 3AB
Tel:(0333) 310628

Scottish Fisheries Museum Trust

Open all year Apr-Oct Mon-Sat 10-5.30 Sun 11-5 Nov-Mar Mon & Sat 10-4.30 Sun 2-4.30. Admission charges (with concessions).
P, ST, <50%, G, C

East end of harbour, parking nearby, refreshments, sales area, temporary exhibitions, wc, parties welcome but must book.

This popular maritime museum is housed in 16th to 19th century buildings typical of the east neuk of Fife. Both the domestic and working life of fishermen and women of the past and present are described. Fine paintings, costume, model boats, domestic objects and tools illustrate all aspects of the Scottish fishing industry. Fishing methods are explained and the marine aquarium is alive with a variety of local fish. Small yawl fishing boats are 'moored' in the courtyard of the museum and examples of the large 'Fifie' and 'Zulu' fishing boats can be seen in the harbour close by. A memorial room dedicated to Scottish fishermen lost at sea reminds visitors of the ever-present dangers of Scottish waters.

BUCKHAVEN

BUCKHAVEN MUSEUM

College Street, Buckhaven, Fife
Correspondence to Kirkcaldy Museum & Art Gallery, War Memorial Gardens, Kirkcaldy, Fife KY1 1YG. Tel:(0592) 260732.

Kirkcaldy District Council

Open all year Mon, Tue, Thu, Fri during library hours including 2-5. Admission free.
P, ST, <50%, G

Town centre, parking for cars & coaches, parties welcome but must book.

A small local museum in a town once described as a 'full flavoured fisher town'. Buckhaven's past importance in the East Coast Fisheries is reflected in the new displays housed above Buckhaven Library.

BURNTISLAND

BURNTISLAND MUSEUM

102 High Street, Burntisland, Fife
Correspondence to Kirkcaldy Art Gallery & Museum, War Memorial Gardens, Kirkcaldy, Fife KY1 1YG. Tel:(0592) 260732.

Kirkcaldy District Council

Open all year Mon-Sat 10-1 & 2-5. Admission free.
PPA, R/ST, 50%, WC, G, C

Town centre, parking for cars, coaches must book, parties welcome but must book.

This museum has recreated a walk through the sights and sounds of the town's fair in 1910, based on a painting of the scene by local artist Andrew Young. Rides, stalls and side-shows of the Edwardian fair. There is also a new local history gallery.

CERES

FIFE FOLK MUSEUM

The Weigh House, Ceres, Cupar, Fife KY15 5NF
Correspondence to A.D. Mackay, Dunviden, Ceres KY15 5LS. Tel:(033 482) 380.

Central & North Fife Preservation Society

Open Apr-Oct Wed-Mon 2.15-5.00. Admission charges.
P, L/R/ST, 50%, G, AD

3 miles from Cupar, parking nearby, sales area, parties welcome, booking preferred.

This popular museum is housed in a unique group of buildings centred on a 17th century tolbooth-weigh house. The adjoining 18th and 19th century pantiled cottages and a new building on the site of a ruined bothy contain a collection based on the social and economic life of Fife. Tools associated with the blacksmith, stonemason, reed thatcher and other trades are on display as well as a cottar's living room and a costume room containing fine gowns, lace and linen. A garden gallery overlooking the Ceres Burn displays agricultural equipment.

Courtyard of the Scottish Fisheries Museum, Anstruther. [*Scottish Fisheries Museum*]

Part of a display on the diversity of human cultures at the Marischal Museum, University of Aberdeen. [*Scottish Museums Council*]

Jo Barker, Artist-in-Residence at Aberdeen Art Gallery in 1988, at work in the Studio Workshop. The tapestry she created was subsequently purchased for the collections by Aberdeen Art Gallery and Museums. [*Mike Davidson/Aberdeen Art Gallery and Museums, Aberdeen City Arts Department*]

CRAIL

CRAIL MUSEUM

64 Marketgate, Crail, Fife KY10 3TL
Tel:(0333) 50869

Crail Preservation Society

Open Easter for two weeks then Jun-mid Sep Mon-Sat 10-12.30 & 2.30-5 Sun 2.30-5. Admission charges.
ST, <50%, G

In village, parking for cars & coaches, sales area, parties welcome but must book.

Local heritage and craft displays telling the story of the Royal Burgh of Crail are included in this small museum, situated in the beautiful East Neuk fishing village.

CULROSS

THE STUDY

The Cross, Culross, Fife
Tel:(0383) 880359

National Trust for Scotland

Open Apr, Jun-Aug, Oct Sat & Sun 2-4. Other times by appointment. Admission charges (with concessions).
ST, <50%, G

12 miles west of Forth Road Bridge off A985, parking for cars & coaches, parties welcome but must book.

Burgh architecture of the 17th century. This building contains reproduction 17th century painted ceilings and 18th century furnishings. Audio-visual programme shown.

THE TOWN HOUSE

Sandhaven, Culross, Fife
Tel:(0383) 880359

National Trust for Scotland

Open Easter & May-Sep daily 11-1 & 2-5. Admission charges (with concessions).
P, ST, <50%, WC, H, G, AD

12 miles west of Forth Road Bridge off A985, parking for cars & coaches, sales area, temporary exhibitions, parties welcome but must book.

Interesting example of a 17th century Scottish burgh house with original painted ceiling, 17th and 18th century furniture, a display of weights and measures from the Royal Burgh of Culross and an audio-visual programme about the history of the town available in several languages for visiting groups.

CUPAR

HILL OF TARVIT MANSION HOUSE

Cupar, Fife
Tel:(0334) 53127

National Trust for Scotland

Open Apr Sat-Sun 2-6, May-Oct daily 2-6. Admission charges (with concessions).
PPA, ST, <50%, WC, G, C

2 1/2 miles south of Cupar off A916, parking for cars & coaches, wc, parties welcome but must book.

This mansion house remodelled in 1906 by Sir Robert Lorimer contains a fascinating collection of tapestries, paintings, furniture, porcelain and 'objets d'art' in an Edwardian setting. The house also contains a fully restored Edwardian kitchen and laundry.

DUNFERMLINE

ANDREW CARNEGIE BIRTHPLACE MUSEUM

Moodie Street, Dunfermline, Fife KY12 7PL
Tel:(0383) 724302
Correspondence to Secretary, Fred Mann, Abbey Park House, Dunfermline, Fife KY12 7PB.

Carnegie Dunfermline Trust

Open all year Apr-Oct Mon-Sat 11-5 Wed 11-8 Sun 2-5 Nov-Mar daily 2-4. Admission free.
P, R, 50%, WC, G

From High Street 400 yds down Guildhall Street, parking nearby, sales area, wc, parties welcome but must book.

Born here in 1835, the weaver's son became a legend in his lifetime. Taken to America as a child, he made an enormous fortune from the steel industry and gave away $350,000,000 to help others. Period furnishings recapture the atmosphere of the cottage and loom shop which Andrew Carnegie knew as a boy. In the Memorial Hall next door, displays tell the story of his remarkable career and show the work of the Trusts he established. The museum offers an audio-visual programme and hologram.

DUNFERMLINE DISTRICT MUSEUM AND SMALL GALLERY

Viewfield Terrace, Dunfermline KY12 7HY
Tel:(0383) 721814

Dunfermline District Council

Open all year Mon-Sat 11-5. Admission free.
P, ST, 50%, G

Town centre, parking nearby, sales area, temporary exhibitions, parties welcome but must book.

The District's main museum has interesting displays of local, social and natural history. Exhibits from the Dunfermline Linen Damask Collection emphasise the importance of the linen industry to the town in the 19th century. The Small Gallery houses art and craft exhibitions which change monthly.

PITTENCRIEFF HOUSE MUSEUM

Pittencrieff Park, Dunfermline, Fife
Tel:(0383) 722935 or 721814
Correspondence to Curator, Dunfermline Museum, Viewfield Terrace, Dunfermline KY12 7HY.
Tel:(0383) 721814.

Dunfermline District Council

Open May-Aug Wed-Mon 11-5. Admission free.
P, R/ST, <50%, G

In park in centre of Dunfermline, parking for cars & coaches, sales area, temporary exhibitions, wc, parties welcome but must book.

Set in beautiful parkland, this elegant 17th century mansion has an important costume collection and an art gallery with a continuous programme of temporary exhibitions as well as local history displays.

DYSART

McDOUALL STUART MUSEUM

Rectory Lane, Dysart, Fife
Correspondence to Kirkcaldy Museum & Art Gallery, War Memorial Gardens, Kirkcaldy, Fife KY1 1YG.
Tel:(0592) 260732

Kirkcaldy District Council

Open Jun-Aug daily 2-5. Admission free.
P, ST, <50%, G

2 miles north of Kirkcaldy off A955, parking for cars & coaches, sales area, parties welcome.

John McDouall Stuart (1815-1866), the first explorer to cross Australia, was born in this house, property of the National Trust for Scotland. The small award-winning museum describes his harrowing journeys and the Australian wilderness. It is the starting point for self-guided tours round this attractive burgh and its historic harbour.

EAST WEMYSS

WEMYSS ENVIRONMENTAL EDUCATION CENTRE

Basement Suite, East Wemyss Primary School, East Wemyss, Fife KY1 4RN
Tel:(0592) 714479

Fife Regional Council

Open all year Mon-Fri 9-4.30, second Sun in Feb-Oct also 2-6. Other times by appointment. Admission free.
PPA, ST, G

East Wemyss on Kirkcaldy to Leven coast road A955, parking for cars, refreshments, sales area, temporary exhibitions, wc, parties welcome but must book.

This small museum within the local school contains displays on the local area including the Wemyss caves, mining, natural history, and everyday artefacts.

FALKLAND

FALKLAND PALACE & GARDEN

Falkland, Fife
Tel:(0337) 57397

National Trust for Scotland

Open Apr-Oct Mon-Sat 10-6 Sun 2-6. Last admission 5. Admission charges (with concessions).
ST, <50%, G

11 miles north of Kirkcaldy on A912, parking for cars & coaches, sales area, wc, parties welcome no need to book.

Attractive 16th century Royal palace containing a reconstructed 17th century king's bedchamber, the Chapel Royal decorated for a visit of Charles I, the original Royal Tennis court, and a collection of important tapestries. The gardens were replanted in 1947 to an early 17th century plan.

GLENROTHES

CORRIDOR GALLERY

Viewfield Road, Glenrothes, Fife KY6 2RA
Tel:(0592) 771700

Fife Regional Council

Open all year daily 9-11. Admission free.
P, L/ST, WC, G, C

South side of town, parking for cars & coaches, refreshments, sales area, temporary exhibitions, wc, parties welcome no need to book.

A small photography gallery situated in a busy public corridor in the Fife Institute of Physical and Recreational Education.

6   Grocer's shop, part of the display 'Changing Times' at Kirkcaldy Museum and Art Gallery.
[Kirkcaldy Museums]

INVERKEITHING

INVERKEITHING MUSEUM

The Friary, Inverkeithing, Fife
Tel:(0383) 413 344
Correspondence to Curator, Dunfermline Museum,
Viewfield Terrace, Dunfermline KY12 7HY.
Tel:(0383) 721 814.

Dunfermline District Council

Open all year Wed-Sun 11-5. Admission free.
PPA, ST, <50%, G

Town centre, parties welcome but must book.

A small museum relating to the history of
Inverkeithing and Rosyth Dockyard. Of
particular interest are items belonging to
Admiral Greig, believed to have founded the
Russian Navy.

KIRKCALDY

KIRKCALDY MUSEUM & ART GALLERY

War Memorial Gardens, Kirkcaldy, Fife KY1 1YG
Tel:(0592) 260732

Kirkcaldy District Council

Open all year Mon-Sat 11-5 Sun 2-5. Admission free.
R, <50%, WC, G, C

Next to Kirkcaldy railway station, parking for cars &
coaches, sales area, temporary exhibitions, wc, parties
welcome no need to book.

Discover the heritage of Kirkcaldy District
through a unique collection of fine Scottish
paintings, fascinating new historical displays
and a full programme of changing art, craft
and local history exhibitions. Special enquiry
and school services available.

LEVEN

LEVEN MUSEUM

Greig Institute, Forth Street, Leven, Fife
Correspondence to Kirkcaldy Museum & Art Gallery,
War Memorial Gardens, Kirkcaldy, Fife KY1 1YG.
Tel:(0592) 260732

Kirkcaldy District Council

Open all year Mon-Sat 10-5. Admission free.
ST, <50%, G

Town centre, parking for cars & coaches, parties
welcome but must book.

This museum above Leven Library contains
photographs and postcards describing the
holiday resort of Leven in Victorian and
Edwardian times.

NEWBURGH

LAING MUSEUM

High Street, Newburgh, Fife KY14 6DX
Tel:(0337) 40223
Correspondence to Curator, North East Fife District
Council Dept. of Recreation, County Buildings,
Cupar, Fife KY15 4TA. Tel:(0334) 53722.

North East Fife District Council

Open Apr-Sep Mon-Fri 11-6 Sat-Sun 2-5, Oct-Mar
Wed, Thu 12-4, Sun 2-5. Admission free.
P, G

Town centre, parking nearby, temporary exhibitions,
parties welcome but must book.

Displays on Victorian Scotland including
emigration, the self-help ethic, the antiquarian
movement and the new sciences. The museum
houses a reconstructed Victorian study and a
historical reference library.

PITTENWEEM

KELLIE CASTLE & GARDEN

Pittenweem, Fife
Tel:(033 38) 271

National Trust for Scotland

Open Apr Sat & Sun 2-6 May-Oct daily 2-6. Last
admission 5.30. Gardens all year. Admission charges
(with concessions).
PPA, L/ST, <50%, H, G, C, AD

3 miles north west of Pittenweem on B9171, parking
for cars & coaches, refreshments, sales area,
temporary exhibitions, wc, parties welcome but must
book.

The castle is a fine example of 16th and 17th
century Lowland Scots architecture,
delightfully furnished in various styles and
retaining a family home atmosphere. The
walled garden is Victorian in design.

LOCHTY PRIVATE RAILWAY

Lochty Farm, Pittenweem, Fife
Tel:(0592) 264587

Fife Railway Preservation Group

Open mid-Jun-1st Sun in Sep Sun only 2-5.30.
Admission charges (with concessions).
P, L, G

On B940 Cupar-Crail road, parking for cars &
coaches, sales area, temporary exhibitions, parties
welcome but must book.

Standard gauge steam railway with a collection
of railway signalling equipment, four steam
locomotives (of the industrial type once used
in Fife), five diesel locomotives, wagons and
four coaches and a Jones KL100 self-propelled
diesel railway crane. A few wheelchairs can be
accommodated on each trip.

ST ANDREWS

BRITISH GOLF MUSEUM

Golf Place, St Andrews, Fife KY16 9JD
Tel:(0334) 73423

Royal & Ancient Golf Club of St Andrews Trust

Open all year May-Oct daily 10-5.30 Nov,Mar,Apr
Tue-Sun 10-5 Dec-Feb Tue-Sat 10-4. Admission
charges (with concessions).
P, R/ST, 100%, WC, G, AD, SL

By 1st tee of The Old Course, parking for cars &
coaches, sales area, wc.

This new museum traces the story of golf from
its misty origins to the present day. Its visual
presentations of objects are complemented by
the use of visitor-activated touch screens
throughout the galleries, using live action
videos, sound commentaries and still pictures
to bring alive historic matches, great golfers of
the past and present, and social changes in the
game. In addition to the main galleries there
is a 50-seat audio-visual theatre which shows
a wide range of golf-related films. A temporary
exhibition area offers constantly changing
exhibitions.

CRAWFORD ARTS CENTRE

93 North Street, St. Andrews, Fife
Tel:(0334) 76161 ex.591

Crawford Arts Centre (St Andrews) Ltd.

Open all year Mon-Sat 10-5 Sun 2-5. Admission free.
PPA, L/ST, 50%, G

Town centre, refreshments, sales area, temporary
exhibitions, wc, parties welcome but must book.

An arts centre with a monthly programme of
temporary exhibitions concentrating on
contemporary work (including photography,
architecture and craftwork) and Scottish art.
Lectures, performing arts and other events are
held throughout the year.

ST. ANDREWS CATHEDRAL

St.Andrews, Fife
Tel:(031) 244 3101 for information

Scottish Development Department (Historic
Buildings and Monuments)

Open Oct-Mar Mon-Sat 9.30-4 Sun 2-4 Apr-Sep
Mon-Sat 9.30-7 Sun 2-7. Admission charges (with
concessions).
ST, G

Centre of town.

Once the largest church in Scotland, the
cathedral is now in ruins. Magnificent displays
of Celtic and medieval monuments, pottery,
glass work and other relics are housed in a
small museum.

ST. ANDREWS PRESERVATION TRUST MUSEUM

12 North Street, St. Andrews, Fife
Tel:(0334) 72152
Correspondence to L. Nash, 115 South Street, St.
Andrews.

St. Andrews Preservation Trust

Open Jul-Aug daily 2-4.30. Admission free.
L, 50%, G

Town centre near Cathedral, parking for cars, sales
area, temporary exhibitions, parties larger than 10
should book.

This reconstructed 17th century house
contains 19th century grocer's and chemist's
shops, burgh weights and measures and aspects
of local life and history. The first floor and
gallery display period furniture, costume,
scrap-books, photographs and topical
temporary displays.

7   Visitors touring the Glenfarclas distillery, Ballindalloch. *[Ken Grant]*

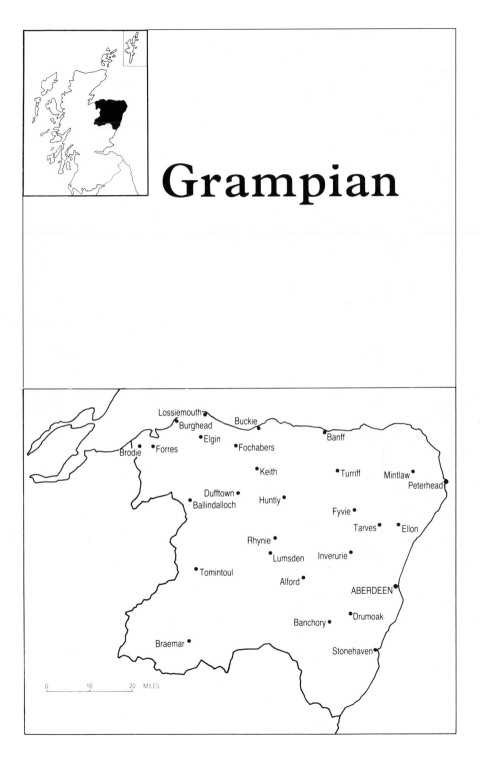

Grampian

Lossiemouth
Burghead
Buckie
Elgin
Banff
Forres
Brodie
Fochabers
Keith
Turriff
Mintlaw
Peterhead
Dufftown
Huntly
Fyvie
Ballindalloch
Tarves
Ellon
Rhynie
Lumsden
Inverurie
Tomintoul
Alford
ABERDEEN
Drumoak
Banchory
Braemar
Stonehaven

0   10   20   MILES

ABERDEEN

ABERDEEN ART GALLERY

Schoolhill, Aberdeen AB9 1FQ
Tel:(0224) 646333

Aberdeen District Council City Arts Department

Open all year Mon-Sat 10-5 Thu 10-8 Sun 2-5.
Admission free.
PPA, R/ST, 100%, WC, G, C

City centre, parking nearby, refreshments, sales area,
temporary exhibitions, wc, parties welcome no need
to book.

The permanent collection is strong in works
by contemporary artists, paintings from the
18th and 19th centuries and fine examples
of North East silver and glass. The gallery
provides a wide-ranging programme of
temporary exhibitions and events, a reference
library and print room.

ABERDEEN ARTS CENTRE GALLERY

King Street, Aberdeen
Tel:(0224) 635208

Aberdeen District Council City Arts Department

Open all year Mon-Sat 10-5. Admission free.
PPA, R/ST, 100%, WC, G, C, B

City centre, parking for cars, refreshments, sales area,
temporary exhibitions, wc, parties welcome no need
to book.

Galleries displaying a changing programme of
exhibitions, concentrating on the works of local
artists and craftsmen.

ABERDEEN MARITIME MUSEUM

Provost Ross's House, Shiprow, Aberdeen AB1 2BY
Tel:(0224) 585788
Correspondence to Aberdeen Art Gallery, Schoolhill,
Aberdeen AB9 1FQ. Tel:(0224) 646333.

Aberdeen District Council City Arts Department

Open all year Mon-Sat 10-5. Admission free.
PPA, L, <50%, WC, G

City centre, parking nearby, sales area, temporary
exhibitions, wc, parties welcome no need to book.

One of the oldest buildings in Aberdeen built
in 1593, the provost's house contains a wide
variety of maritime displays including local
shipbuilding, Arctic whaling, the fishing
industry, north boats, wrecks and rescues,
London boats and North Sea oil and gas. The
building also houses a National Trust Shop
and Information Centre which is open from
May-September and for three weeks before
Christmas.

BLAIRS COLLEGE MUSEUM

Blairs College, Aberdeen AB9 2LA
Tel:(0224) 867626 or 861177

Blairs College Trustees

Open last Sat of month 2-5. Other times by
appointment. Admission free.
ST, <50%, G

4 miles from Aberdeen on South Deeside Road,
parking for cars & coaches, temporary exhibitions,
wc, parties welcome but must book.

Contains major pictures of Mary Queen of
Scots, among them her memorial portrait and
miniature in reliquary (Blairs Jewel). The
museum has Stuart portraits and memorabilia,
16th century Church robes and a collection of
altarware on display.

GORDON HIGHLANDERS' REGIMENTAL MUSEUM

Viewfield Road, Aberdeen
Tel:(0224) 318174

Gordon Highlanders' Regimental Trust

Closed 1990 for cataloguing. Opening times thereafter
subject to review. Admission free.
PPA, L/R, 50%, G

On A944, parking for cars, sales area, parties welcome
but must book.

Relics tracing the history of the regiment
from its formation in 1794. General militaria
including medals, uniforms, albums and
scrapbooks.

JAMES DUN'S HOUSE

Schoolhill, Aberdeen AB1 1JT
Tel:(0224) 646333
Correspondence to Aberdeen Art Gallery, Schoolhill,
Aberdeen AB9 1FQ. Tel:(0224) 646333.

Aberdeen District Council City Arts Department

Open all year Mon-Sat 10-5. Admission free.
PPA, ST, <50%, G

City centre, parking nearby, sales area, temporary
exhibitions, wc, parties welcome no need to book.

An 18th century town house renovated for use
as a museum with permanent displays and
special exhibitions.

MARISCHAL MUSEUM

Marischal College, Broad Street, Aberdeen AB9 1AS
Tel:(0224) 273131

University of Aberdeen

Open all year Mon-Fri 10-5 Sun 2-5. Admission free.
<50%, G, C

City centre, sales area, temporary exhibitions, wc,
parties welcome but must book.

Exhibits range from items of local archaeology (including Bronze Age burials) and collections from ancient Egypt and the South Sea Islands to art and antiquities from Europe, Asia, Africa, America and the Pacific. A new display, 'Encyclopaedia of the North East' opens in early 1990.

NATURAL HISTORY MUSEUM

Department of Zoology, University of Aberdeen, Tillydrone Avenue, Aberdeen AB9 2TN
Tel:(0224) 272849 or 275850

Department of Zoology

Open all year Mon-Fri 9-5. Admission free.
P, L/R/ST, 50%, G

On ring road to Peterhead in Old Aberdeen, parking for cars, temporary exhibitions, wc, not suitable for parties.

Collection of invertebrates and vertebrates primarily for undergraduate teaching housed in a modern gallery.

PEACOCK ARTSPACE

21 Castle Street, Aberdeen AB1 1AJ
Tel:(0224) 639539

Peacock Printmakers

Open all year Mon-Sat 9.30-5. Admission free.
PPA, L/R, 50%, WC, G, AD

City centre, parking for cars, sales area, temporary exhibitions, wc, parties welcome but must book.

The Museum of Printing History will be a permanent display explaining major printing processes, placing them in a historic context. A wide selection of prints by Scottish artists on permanent display in shop.

PROVOST SKENE'S HOUSE

Guestrow, off Broad Street, Aberdeen AB1 1AR
Tel:(0224) 641086
Correspondence to Aberdeen Art Gallery, Schoolhill, Aberdeen AB9 1FQ. Tel:(0224) 646333.

Aberdeen District Council City Arts Department

Open all year Mon-Sat 10-5. Admission free.
PPA, R, <50%, G, C

City centre, parking nearby, refreshments, sales area, wc, parties welcome no need to book.

A 17th century furnished town house with period rooms, displays of local history and an outstanding painted ceiling from about 1630. Provost Skene's Kitchen is open for tea, coffee and light meals.

SAINT ANDREWS CATHEDRAL

28 King Street, Aberdeen AB2 3AX
Tel:(0224) 640290
Correspondence to A.C. Stuart Donald, 45 Beaconsfield Place, Aberdeen AB2 2AB.

The Trustees

Open May-Sep Mon-Sat 10-4. Admission free.
P, R, 100%, WC, G, C, AD, SL

Town centre, parking for cars, coaches must book, refreshments, sales area, wc, parties welcome no need to book.

The Cathedral contains the Seabury Memorial commemorating the Consecration of Samuel Seabury of Connecticut in Aberdeen in 1784 as the first Bishop of America and of the Anglican Communion outside the British Isles. A permanent exhibition, 'The Christian heritage of the North East of Scotland' provides an ecumenical description of the history of the Christian church in the area.

SATROSPHERE

19 Justice Mill Lane, Aberdeen AB1 2EQ
Tel:(0224) 213232

Science and Technology Regional Office - North of Scotland

Open all year Wed-Sun 10-4. Admission charges (with concessions).
PPA, R/ST, 100%, WC, C

Town centre, parking nearby, refreshments, sales area, wc.

An interactive science and technology exhibition, opened in February 1990. Visitors can try out experiments with light, heat, and sound and all exhibits can be touched. Helpers stationed throughout the displays explain the working exhibits and experiments you can carry out.

ALFORD

ALFORD-DONSIDE HERITAGE CENTRE

Mart Road, Alford, Aberdeenshire AB3 8AA.
Tel:(09755) 62221
Correspondence to Mr H Fraser, Marchmont, Keig, Alford, Aberdeenshire AB3 8BH. Tel:(09755)62701.

Alford and Donside Heritage Association

Open Apr-Sep Mon-Sat 10-9 Sun 1-9. Admission charges (with concessions).
P, L, 100%, WC, G

Village centre, parking for cars & coaches, wc, parties welcome booking preferred.

A small local history museum, with agricultural displays. Guided tours and country walks available for parties.

CRAIGIEVAR CASTLE

Alford, Aberdeenshire
Tel:(033 983) 635

National Trust for Scotland

Open May-Jun, Sep daily 2-6. Last admission 5.15. Groups at other times by appointment. Admission charges (with concessions).
P, ST, <50%, G

6 miles south of Alford & 26 miles west of Aberdeen on A980, parking for cars & coaches, sales area, wc, parties welcome but must book.

A magnificent example of the Scottish tower house of the early 17th century with many impressive moulded Renaissance ceilings. The contents of this historic house are best described as a family collection which began in the 17th century.

GRAMPIAN TRANSPORT MUSEUM & RAILWAY MUSEUM

Alford, Aberdeenshire AB3 8AD
Tel:(09755) 62292

Independent

Open Apr-Sep daily 10.30-5. Other times by appointment. Admission charges (with concessions).
P, L, <50%, WC, G

23 miles west of Aberdeen on A944, parking for cars & coaches, refreshments, sales area, temporary exhibitions, wc, parties welcome but must book.

The site contains two museums - transport and railway. The larger transport museum concentrates on the transport history of the North East and has a vast collection of vehicles including steam wagons and traction engines, lorries, fire engines, buses, trams, horse-drawn, motor cars, motor cycles and cycles. The Craigievar Express, a unique survivor from the dawn of the motoring era, built by an inventive local postman, is just one of the displays. The adjacent railway museum occupies the site of the former GNSR Alford Station and features exhibits on the history of the railway. There is a passenger carrying narrow gauge line which takes visitors through the nearby country park.

BALLINDALLOCH

GLENFARCLAS DISTILLERY

Ballindalloch, Banffshire AB3 9BD
Tel:(080 72) 245

J & G Grant

Open all year Mon-Fri 9-4.30 Jun-Sep also Sat 9-4.30 Sun 1-4. Admission free.
P, L/R, 50%, WC, G, B, AD

18 miles from Elgin on A95, parking for cars & coaches, sales area, wc, parties welcome but please book.

Mementoes, photographs and equipment of the Glenfarclas Distillery and the Grant family are on display. An exhibition describes the making of whisky. A filling store/cooperage allows visitors to view new whisky going into oak casks to begin maturation. Free guided tour and complimentary dram.

BANCHORY

BANCHORY MUSEUM

Burgh Buildings, High Street, Banchory
Correspondence to Museums Curator, Arbuthnot Museum, Peterhead AB4 6QD. Tel:(0779) 77778.

North East of Scotland Museums Service

Open Jun-Sep Fri-Wed 2-5.15. Admission free.
PPA, ST, 100%, G

Town centre, parking for cars, sales area, temporary exhibitions, parties welcome but must book.

A small but interesting local history museum with items associated with Scott Skinner 'The Strathspey King'.

CRATHES CASTLE

Banchory, Kincardineshire AB3 3QJ
Tel:(033 044) 525

National Trust for Scotland

Open Easter & May-Sep Mon-Sat 11-6 Sun 2-6. Last admission 5.15. Admission charges (with concessions).
PPA, L/R, <50%, WC, G, C, B

3 miles east of Banchory & 15 miles west of Aberdeen on A93, parking for cars & coaches, refreshments, sales area, wc, parties welcome but must book.

The 16th century home of the Burnetts of Leys contains remarkable painted ceilings and some original Scottish vernacular furniture. The garden is a composite of eight separate gardens with great yew hedges dating from 1702. The grounds contain several nature trails, including one long-distance.

8   The Craigievar Express, a unique steam-powered motorised tricycle built by a local 'postie' in the late 19th century and now in the collections of the Grampian Transport Museum, Alford.
[Grampian Transport Museum]

BANFF

BANFF MUSEUM

High Street, Banff, Banffshire
Correspondence to Museums Curator, Arbuthnot Museum, Peterhead AB4 6QD. Tel:(0779) 77778.

North East of Scotland Museums Service

Open Jun-Sep Fri-Wed 2-5.15. Admission free. L, 50%

Town centre, parking nearby, sales area, parties welcome but must book.

A local museum with material relating to the social and natural history of the town and immediate district. Collections include scientific instruments which belonged to the astronomer James Ferguson and the natural history collection of Thomas Edward.

BRAEMAR

BRAEMAR CASTLE

Braemar, by Ballater, Aberdeenshire AB3 5XR
Tel:(03383) 219

Captain A.C. Farquharson of Invercauld MC

Open May-first Mon in Oct daily 10-6. Admission charges.

1/2 mile north east of Braemar on A93, parking for cars & coaches, sales area, wc, parties welcome booking preferred.

An impressive fortress of fairy-tale proportions originally built in 1628 but substantially altered in 1748. Now furnished as a private residence, the castle contains some fine antiques, paintings and family relics. A large Cairngorm, a semi-precious stone weighing 52lbs. and understood to be the largest in existence in its natural state, is on permanent display. The castle also contains a massive iron 'yett' and an underground prison.

BRODIE

BRODIE CASTLE

Brodie
Tel:(030 94) 371

National Trust for Scotland

Open Apr-Sep Mon-Sat 11-6 Sun 2-6 Oct Sat 11-6 Sun 2-6. Admission charges (with concessions).
PPA, L/ST, 50%, WC, G, AD, SL

4 1/2 miles west of Forres & 24 miles east of Inverness off A96, parking for cars & coaches, refreshments, sales area, wc, parties welcome but must book.

Ancient home of the Brodies of Brodie housing a fine collection of paintings, French furniture and 17th century plasterwork.

BUCKIE

BUCKIE MARITIME MUSEUM & PETER ANSON GALLERY

Townhouse, West Cluny Place, Buckie, Moray AB5 1HB
Correspondence to Falconer Museum, Tolbooth Street, Forres, Moray IV36 OPH. Tel:(0309) 73701.

Moray District Council

Open all year Mon-Fri 10-8 Sat 10-12. Admission free.
PPA, 100%, G

Town centre (Buckie - Elgin coastal route), parking for cars, sales area, temporary exhibitions, parties welcome but must book.

Emphasising Buckie's strong connection with the sea, this interesting museum tells the story of fishing in the town from 1800 to the present day. The adjoining gallery, a memorial to Peter Anson, displays a selection from the museum's extensive collection of the artist's work.

DRUMOAK

DRUM CASTLE

Drumoak, by Banchory, Aberdeenshire
Tel:(033 08) 204

National Trust for Scotland

Open mid Apr-Sep daily 2-6 Oct Sat & Sun 2-6. Last admission 5.15. Admission charges (with concessions).
PPA, ST, 50%, G, C

3 miles west of Peterculter & 10 miles west of Aberdeen off A93, parking for cars & coaches, refreshments, wc, parties welcome but must book.

This late 13th century tower house with 17th and 19th century additions is the home of the Irvines of Drum. The house contains good Georgian furniture, needlework, family portraits, blue and white ware and a Victorian kitchen.

DUFFTOWN

DUFFTOWN MUSEUM

The Tower, The Square, Dufftown, Moray AB5 4AD
Correspondence to Falconer Museum, Tolbooth Street, Forres, Moray IV36 OPH. Tel:(0309) 73701.

Moray District Council

Open May,Jun,Sep Mon-Sat 9.30-5.30 Jul & Aug Mon-Sat 9.30-6.30 Sun 2-6.30. Admission free.
L, 100%, G

Town centre, sales area, temporary exhibitions, parties welcome but must book.

Housed in the same building as the Tourist Information Centre, this small museum illustrates the history of Dufftown and of Mortlach Church.

ELGIN

ELGIN MUSEUM

1 High Street, Elgin IV30 1EQ
Tel:(0343) 543675

Moray Society

Open Easter-Oct Tue-Sat 10-5 Sun 2-7. Admission charges (with concessions).
R, 50%, WC, G

Town centre, parking for cars, sales area, wc, parties welcome no need to book.

An interesting local museum begun in 1836 with some notable collections of archaeology, including Pictish stones, natural history, social history and an internationally important collection of fossils which includes the Elgin Reptiles.

ELLON

PITMEDDEN MUSEUM, GARDEN & GROUNDS

Ellon, Aberdeenshire AB4 0PD
Tel:(065 13) 2352

National Trust for Scotland

Museum open May-Sep daily 10-6. Last admission 5.15. Garden & grounds all year daily 9.30-sunset. Admission charges (with concessions).
PPA, L, 100%, WC, G, C

14 miles north west of Aberdeen off A920, parking for cars & coaches, refreshments, wc, parties welcome but must book.

An exhibition on the history of gardening in Scotland and a museum of farming life are closely attached to Pitmedden Garden, an elaborate reconstruction of a 17th century formal garden with parterres.

FOCHABERS

FOCHABERS FOLK MUSEUM

Pringle Antiques, High Street, Fochabers, Moray

Christies (Fochabers) Ltd.

Open all year 9.30-5.00. Admission charges (with concessions).
P, L, 50%, G, C

On A96 in Fochabers, parking for cars & coaches, refreshments, sales area, parties welcome no need to book.

The museum is housed in a former church. On the top floor there are 16 gigs and carts. On the ground floor there are many items concerned with bygone days in Fochabers and the surrounding area including a complete village shop.

TUGNET ICE HOUSE

Tugnet, Spey Bay, Fochabers, Moray
Correspondence to Falconer Museum, Tolbooth Street, Forres, Moray IV36 OPH. Tel:(0309) 73701.

Moray District Council

Open Jun-Sep daily 9-5. Admission free.
P, L, 100%, WC, G, AD

At end of B9104 at mouth of Spey, parking for cars & coaches, sales area, wc, parties welcome but must book.

This restored ice house, previously used for storing salmon, contains displays on salmon fishing on the Spey and on the history, wildlife, geology and climate of the surrounding area. Audio-visual programme on the River Spey.

FORRES

FALCONER MUSEUM

Tolbooth Street, Forres, Moray IV36 OPH
Tel:(0309) 73701

Moray District Council

Open May,Jun,Sep,Oct Mon-Sat 10-12.30 & 1.30-5.30 Jul,Aug Mon-Sat 9.30-12.30 & 1.30-6.30 Sun 2-5 Nov-Apr Mon-Fri 10-12.30 & 1.30-4.30. Admission free.
PPA, L, 50%, G

Town centre, parking for cars & coaches, sales area, temporary exhibitions, parties welcome but must book.

Museum of local and natural history with many exhibits and pictures of Forres and its area. 'The Story of Forres', 'Hugh Falconer-Palaeontologist', 'Local Birds and Animals' are amongst the permanent displays. Temporary exhibitions are held regularly.

FYVIE

FYVIE CASTLE

Fyvie, Aberdeenshire
Tel:(065 16) 226

National Trust for Scotland

Castle open May-Sep daily 2-6. Last admission 5.15. Grounds open all year. Admission charges (with concessions).
PPA, L, <50%, WC, G, C

8 miles south east of Turriff off A947, parking for cars & coaches, refreshments, temporary exhibitions, wc, parties welcome but must book.

The five towers of Fyvie enshrine five centuries of Scottish history, each being built by one of the five families who owned the castle. The oldest part dates from the 13th century and is now probably the grandest example of Scottish baronial architecture. The interior as created by the first Lord Leith of Fyvie reflects the opulence of the Edwardian era. The house contains arms and armour, 16th century tapestries and an important collection of portraits including works by Batoni, Raeburn, Ramsay and Gainsborough.

HUNTLY

BRANDER MUSEUM

The Square, Huntly, Aberdeenshire
Correspondence to Museums Curator, Arbuthnot Museum, Peterhead AB4 6QD. Tel:(0779) 77778.

North East of Scotland Museums Service

Open all year Tue-Sat 10-12 & 2-4. Admission free.
PPA, ST, 100%, G

Town centre, parking nearby, sales area, temporary exhibitions, parties welcome but must book.

Housed in the local library, this collection of local history material contains archaeological finds of national importance.

LEITH HALL

Kennethmont, Huntly, Aberdeenshire
Tel:(046 43) 216

National Trust for Scotland

Open May-Sep daily 2-6. Last admission 5.15. Admission charges (with concessions).
P, L, <50%, WC, G, C

1 mile west of Kennethmont & 7 miles south west of Huntly on B9002, parking for cars & coaches, refreshments, wc, parties welcome but must book.

The home of the Leith family since the mid-17th century, built around a central courtyard, contains fine examples of 18th century furniture, family portraits and a collection of militaria from the family's history. Exhibition 'For Crown and Country: The Military Lairds of Leith Hall'.

INVERURIE

CARNEGIE MUSEUM

Town Hall, The Square, Inverurie, Aberdeenshire
Correspondence to Museums Curator, Arbuthnot Museum, Peterhead AB4 6QD. Tel:(0779) 77778.

North East of Scotland Museums Service

Open all year Mon-Fri 2-5 Sat 10-12. Admission free.
ST, G

Near station, parking nearby, sales area, temporary exhibitions, parties welcome but must book.

Predominantly a local history museum, collections also include archaeological material and Eskimo carvings of international importance. There is a display of railway (GNSR) memorabilia and temporary exhibitions change regularly.

CASTLE FRASER

Sauchen, Inverurie, Aberdeenshire
Tel:(033 03) 463

National Trust for Scotland

Open May-Sep daily 2-6. Last admission 5.15. Admission charges (with concessions).
PPA, L/ST, <50%, G, C

16 miles west of Aberdeen & 3 miles south of Kemnay off B993, parking for cars & coaches, refreshments, wc, parties welcome but must book.

An outstanding tower house, once the home of the Fraser family. Contents include some early oak furniture and portraits dating from the 17th to the 19th centuries.

LOSSIEMOUTH

LOSSIEMOUTH FISHERIES AND COMMUNITY MUSEUM

Pitgaveny Street, Lossiemouth

Lossiemouth Community Council

Open Easter-Sep Mon-Fri 10-4.30 Sat 10-1. Admission charges (with concessions).
P, L/ST, 50%, WC, AD

In town, parking for cars & coaches, sales area, parties welcome but must book.

A community museum overlooking the harbour, which tells the story of the local fishing industry.

LUMSDEN

SCOTTISH SCULPTURE WORKSHOP

1 Main Street, Lumsden, by Huntly, Aberdeenshire
Tel:(046 46) 372

Scottish Sculpture Workshop

Open all year daily 10-4. Admission free.
P, L, 100%

35 miles west of Aberdeen on Aberdeen - Alford/Huntly Road, parking for cars & coaches, sales area, temporary exhibitions, wc, parties welcome but must book.

Small gallery used primarily to show sculptures made on the premises.

MINTLAW

DEER ABBEY

Mintlaw, Aberdeenshire
Tel:(031) 244 3101 for information.

Scottish Development Department (Historic Buildings and Monuments)

Open Apr-Sep Thu-Sat 9.30-7 Sun 2-7. Admission charges (with concessions).
G

Near Old Deer 10 miles west of Peterhead.

The remains of a Cistercian abbey founded in 1218. The small site museum displays some interesting pieces of masonry.

NORTH EAST OF SCOTLAND AGRICULTURAL HERITAGE CENTRE

Aden Country Park, Mintlaw, nr. Peterhead, Aberdeenshire AB4 8LD
Tel:(0771) 22857

Banff & Buchan District Council

Open May-Sep daily 11-5. Apr & Oct Sat,Sun 12-5. Admission free.
P, R, 50%, WC, G, C, AD

30 miles north of Aberdeen & 1 mile west of Mintlaw on A950, parking for cars & coaches, refreshments, wc, parties welcome but must book.

Housed in the carefully restored Aden Home Farm, the Centre interprets 20th century estate life through an audiovisual programme, reconstructed horseman's house and costumed guides. North East farming life and innovation over 200 years are highlighted in the 'Weel Vrocht Grun' (well worked ground) exhibition by use of dioramas, atmospheric soundtrack and video film.

9 Aden Home Farm, which houses the North East of Scotland Agricultural Heritage Centre at Mintlaw. *[North East of Scotland Agricultural Heritage Centre]*

PETERHEAD

ARBUTHNOT MUSEUM

St. Peter Street, Peterhead, Aberdeenshire AB4 6QD
Tel:(0779) 77778

North East of Scotland Museums Service

Open all year Mon-Sat 10-12 & 2-5. Admission free.
ST, G

Town centre, parking nearby, sales area, temporary exhibitions, parties welcome but must book.

Headquarters of the North East of Scotland Museums Service, this local history museum contains displays and exhibits relating to Peterhead's past and the town's connection with the whaling industry. Collections include Eskimo artefacts of international interest and coins.

STONEHAVEN

TOLBOOTH MUSEUM

The Harbour, Stonehaven, Kincardineshire
Correspondence to Museums Curator, Arbuthnot Museum, Peterhead AB4 6QD. Tel:(0779) 77778.

North East of Scotland Museums Service

Open Jun-Sep Mon,Thu,Fri,Sat 10-12 & 2-5
Wed,Sun 2-5. Admission free.
PPA, L, 50%, G

Parking nearby, sales area, temporary exhibitions, parties welcome but must book.

This small museum in the 16th century former tolbooth contains displays of local history.

10   Haddo House, the William Adam-designed Georgian home of the Gordons, Earls and Marquesses of Aberdeen. *[National Trust for Scotland]*

TARVES

HADDO HOUSE

Tarves, Aberdeenshire
Tel:(065 15) 440

National Trust for Scotland

Open mid Apr-Oct daily 2-6. Last admission 5.15. Country park & garden all year daily 9.30-sunset. Admission charges (with concessions).
P, L, 50%, WC, G, C

4 miles north of Pitmedden & 19 miles north of Aberdeen off B999, parking for cars & coaches, refreshments, sales area, wc, parties welcome but must book.

Family home of the Gordons, Earls and Marquesses of Aberdeen, built by William Adam in the 1730s and remodelled in the 1880s. Relics of the family are on display, including a specially hand-painted dinner service presented by the women of Canada to the first Marquess who was Governor General of Canada from 1893 to 1898.

TOMINTOUL

TOMINTOUL VISITOR CENTRE

The Square, Tomintoul, Moray AB3 9ET
Correspondence to Falconer Museum, Tolbooth Street, Forres, Moray IV36 OPH. Tel:(0309) 73701.

Moray District Council

Open Apr,May,Oct Mon-Sat 9-5.30 Jun,Sep Mon-Sat 9-6 Sun 2-6 Jul,Aug Mon-Sat 9-7 Sun 11-7. Admission free.
P, L, 100%, G

Town centre, parking for cars & coaches, sales area, temporary exhibitions, parties welcome but must book.

A reconstructed farmhouse kitchen provides a focal point for this museum which also has displays on peat-cutting, climatology, landscape, geology, wildlife and the history of the area.

TURRIFF

SESSION COTTAGE MUSEUM

Castlehill, Turriff, Aberdeenshire
Correspondence to Anna Cormack, Kemeri, 22 Westfield Road, Turriff AB5 7AF.

Turriff & District Heritage Society

Open Jun Thu,Sat 2.30-4.30 Jul, Aug Tue,Thu,Sat 2.30-4.30. Admission charges.
P, R, 100%, G

In village, parking for cars & coaches, temporary exhibitions, wc, parties welcome but must book.

A 250 year old 'but n'ben' cottage furnished as a home of about a century ago.

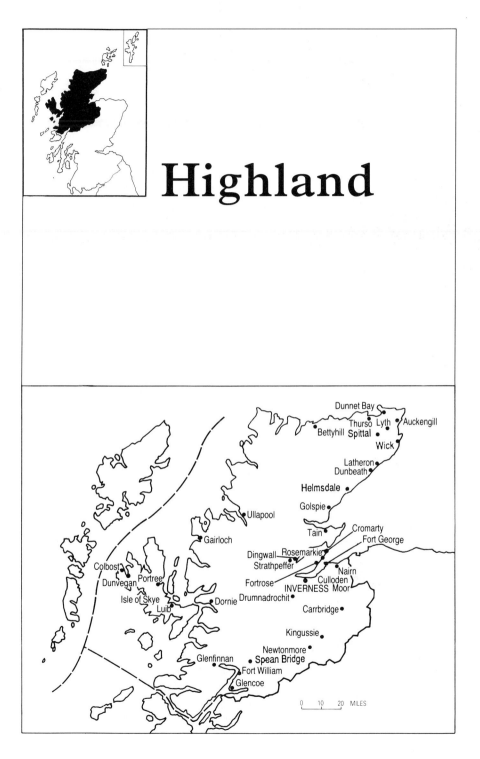

Highland

ACHNACARRY

CLAN CAMERON MUSEUM

Achnacarry, Spean Bridge, Inverness-shire
Tel:(0397) 772 473

Clan Cameron Charitable Trust

Open daily mid Apr-mid Oct 2-5. Other times by appointment. Admission charges (with concessions).
P, R, 100%, WC, G

7 miles from Spean Bridge on B8004 to Loch Arkaig, parking for cars & coaches, sales area, wc.

This museum shows the history of the Cameron Clan at Achnacarry and their involvement in the Bonnie Prince Charlie rising. There are sections on the Queen's Own Cameron Highlanders and the Commandos, who trained at Achnacarry during the last war. A small shop is also in the building which was reconstructed on the site of the croft which was set on fire by the soldiery in the '45.

ARDERSIER

QUEEN'S OWN HIGHLANDERS' REGIMENTAL MUSEUM

Fort George, Ardersier, Inverness-shire
Tel:(0463) 224380

Queen's Own Highlanders

Open all year Apr-Sep Mon-Sat 10-6 Sun 2-6 Oct-Mar Mon-Fri 10-4. Admission free but charge for entry to Fort George.
PPA, L, <50%

15 miles east of Inverness, parking for cars & coaches, sales area, wc, parties welcome no need to book.

A display of uniforms, weapons, pictures, medals, colours, pipe banners, trophies etc. (1778 to the present day) from the 72nd Highlanders, 78th Highlanders, Seaforth Highlanders, 79th Cameron Highlanders, Queen's Own Cameron Highlanders, Queen's Own Highlanders, Lovat Scouts, Militia, Volunteers and Territorial Army. The fort is Ministry of Defence property under the care of the Scottish Development Department and is still in use as barracks for an infantry battalion.

AUCKENGILL

JOHN NICOLSON MUSEUM

Auckengill, Caithness
Correspondence to Caithness Museum Service, Leisure and Recreation Department, Council Offices, Market Square, Wick KW1 4AB. Tel:(0955) 3761.

Caithness District Council

Open Jun-Aug Mon-Sat 10-12 & 2-4. Groups at other times by appointment. Admission charges (with concessions).
P, R, 100%, WC, G

10 miles north of Wick on the A9, parking for cars & coaches, sales area, wc, parties welcome no need to book.

The museum houses displays on the archaeological history of the county and the life and works of John Nicolson, a local antiquarian. Future plans include an audio-visual programme and the building of a replica broch and Viking longhouse in an area behind the museum.

BETTYHILL

STRATHNAVER MUSEUM

Clachan, Bettyhill, by Thurso KW14 7SQ
Tel:(064 12) 330

Correspondence to Mrs. Rudie, Ardveg, Bettyhill, Sutherland.

Trustees of Strathnaver Museum

Open Apr-Sep Mon-Sat 10-1 & 2-5. Admission charges.
P, L/ST, 50%, G

30 miles west of Thurso on A836, parking for cars & coaches, sales area, temporary exhibitions, wc, parties welcome no need to book.

Once a church, this highland museum contains a fine collection of objects depicting a past way of life in this remote but magnificent part of Scotland. One room contains Clan Mackay memorabilia. Posters painted by local children tell the story of the Strathnaver clearances. The churchyard contains the Farr Stone which dates from the 8th-9th centuries.

CARRBRIDGE

LANDMARK

Carrbridge, Inverness-shire PH23 3AJ
Tel:(047 984) 613

Private

Open all year winter 9.30-5.30, summer 9.30-8.30. Admission charges.
P, R, 100%, WC, G, C, B

6 miles north of Aviemore on A9, parking for cars & coaches, refreshments, sales area, temporary exhibitions, wc, parties welcome, booking preferred.

Europe's first visitor centre, Landmark was opened in 1970. A three-screen multi-vision show together with an exhibition presents the story of the Highlander. The pine woods surrounding the centre contain tree top trail and nature trail, pinewood nature centre, giant adventure playground, woodland maze.

Landmark is also the home of the Scottish Forestry Heritage Park telling the story of Scotland's timber industry. Attractions include a 65 feet viewing tower, working steam powered sawmill, exhibitions and demonstrations.

CROMARTY

CROMARTY COURTHOUSE

Church Street, Cromarty, Ross-shire
Tel:(038 17) 243

Cromarty Courthouse Trust

Opening Easter 1991. Easter-end Sept daily. Admission charges (with concessions).

Town centre, sales area, wc.

A new museum telling the story of Cromarty's important role in the history of Scotland.

HUGH MILLER'S COTTAGE

Church Street, Cromarty, Ross-shire
Tel:(038 17) 245

National Trust for Scotland

Open mid Apr-Sep Mon-Sat 10-12 & 1-5 Sun 2-5. Admission charges (with concessions).
ST, <50%, G

22 miles north east of Inverness via Kessock Bridge & A832, parking for cars & coaches, parties welcome but must book.

Built in 1711, this cottage was the home of Hugh Miller, geologist and writer (1802-1852). It is appropriately furnished and displays examples of his fossil collection. The cottage garden has been redeveloped in keeping with the period.

CULLODEN MOOR

CULLODEN VISITOR CENTRE

Culloden Moor, Inverness-shire
Tel:(0463) 790607

National Trust for Scotland

Open Apr-May & Sep-Oct daily 9.30-5.30 Jun-Sep daily 9-7.30. Last admission 1/2 hour before closing. Admission charges (with concessions).
P, WC, H

5 miles east of Inverness on B9006, parking for cars & coaches, refreshments, sales area, wc, parties welcome no need to book.

The main centre on the site of the Battle of Culloden (1746) has been enlarged and improved to include a colourful historical display, audio-visual programme (in English, French, German and Gaelic), auditorium and study room. Relics of the battle are on display in Old Leanach Cottage nearby.

DINGWALL

DINGWALL MUSEUM

Town Hall, Dingwall, Ross-shire
Correspondence to Hon. Secretary, Dr A A Woodham, Scardroy, Greenhill St, Dingwall V15 9NG. Tel:(0349) 62116.

Dingwall Museum Trust

Open May-Sep Mon-Sat 10-5. Admission charges (with concessions).
L, 100%, G

Centre of Dingwall 14 miles north of Inverness, parking for cars & coaches, sales area, small parties welcome no need to book.

This recently refurbished local history museum contains relics and mementoes of past life in Dingwall and district, including military exhibits.

DORNIE

EILEAN DONAN CASTLE MUSEUM

Dornie, Kyle of Lochalsh
Tel:(0599 85) 202

The Conchra Charitable Trust

Open Easter-Sep daily 10-12.30 & 2-6. Admission charges.
ST, 100%, G

At meeting point of Lochs Duich, Long & Alsh, parking for cars & coaches, sales area, temporary exhibitions, wc, parties welcome no need to book.

This beautiful Seaforth castle, set in mountainous countryside, was built originally in 1220, destroyed in 1719 after being held by Jacobite troups and restored in 1912. It contains Clan MacRae relics.

DRUMNADROCHIT

LOCH NESS MONSTER EXHIBITION

Drumnadrochit, Inverness-shire
Tel:(04562) 573

Private

Open all year daily 10-5 mid season 9.30-6 peak season 9-9.30. Admission charges (with concessions).
P, R, 100%, WC, G, C, B, AD

11   Display on wool spinning, weaving and dyeing at Gairloch Heritage Museum, Gairloch.
[Gairloch Heritage Museum]

15 miles from Inverness on A82, parking for cars & coaches, refreshments, sales area, wc, parties welcome no need to book.

A multi-media display relating to the elusive Loch Ness Monster.

DUNBEATH

LHAIDHAY CROFT MUSEUM

Dunbeath, Caithness KW6 6EH
Tel:(059 32) 208

Lhaidhay Preservation Trust

Open Easter-Sep daily 9-6. Admission charges.
P, L, G

20 miles south of Wick on A9, parking for cars & coaches, wc, parties welcome but must book.

A typical 19th century croft with accomodation for animals and a 'cruck' framed barn, this museum contains a display of interesting examples of contemporary literature, early agricultural implements and machinery. A picnic area is adjacent.

DUNNET BAY

DUNNET PAVILION

Dunnet Bay, Caithness KW14 8XD
Correspondence to Libraries & Leisure Services Dept., Highland Regional Council, Kinmylies Building, Leachkin Road, Inverness IV6 3NN.

Highland Regional Council

Open   Apr-Sep   Tue,Wed,Fri,Sat,Sun   10-5.
Admission free.
P, ST, G

8 miles east of Thurso, parking for cars & coaches, wc, parties welcome no need to book.

The display at Dunnet describes the natural history and geology of the area providing a starting point for walks and explorations of Caithness. Two sea-water aquaria contain rock-pool creatures and local sea-shells. Children are encouraged to bring in their own shells and objects for identification and to look at their finer details using a simple microscope.

FORT WILLIAM

WEST HIGHLAND MUSEUM

Cameron Square, Fort William PH33 6AJ
Tel:(0397) 2169

Trustees of the West Highland Museum

Open all year Mon-Sat Jun & Sep 9.30-5.30 Jul &
Aug 9.30-9 Oct-May 10-1 & 2-5. Admission charges
(with concessions).
P, ST, <50%, G

Town centre, parking for cars & coaches, sales area,
wc, parties welcome in small groups, schools must
book.

All aspects of the district's history are shown
in interesting displays of archaeology, natural
history, weapons and domestic utensils. Relics
from the 1745 Jacobite rising on display include
a secret portrait of Prince Charles Edward
Stuart.

FORTROSE

FORTROSE TOWN HALL

Station Road, Fortrose, Ross & Cromarty IP10 8TE
Tel:(0381) 20797
Correspondence to Museums Curator, Ross &
Cromarty District Council, County Buildings,
Dingwall.

Ross & Cromarty District Council

Open all year Mon-Fri 9.30-4.30. Keys can be
obtained from District Office, Cathedral Square,
Fortrose. Admission free.
P, R, 100%, G

Off main street, parking for cars & coaches, wc,
parties welcome but must book.

A collection of portraits of the Seaforth family,
originally from Brahan Castle.

GAIRLOCH

GAIRLOCH HERITAGE MUSEUM

Gairloch, Ross-shire
Tel:(044 583) 243

Gairloch & District Heritage Society

Open Easter-Sep Mon-Sat 10-5. Admission charges.
P, 100%, G, C

Centre of Gairloch of A832, parking for cars &
coaches, refreshments, sales area, parties welcome no
need to book.

An interesting and enjoyable folk museum
depicting the way of life in Gairloch parish
from prehistory to the present. A room
furnished as an old croft and the two locally
built fishing boats outside are of special
interest. A licensed restaurant is attached.

GLENCOE

GLENCOE & NORTH LORN FOLK MUSEUM

Glencoe Village, Argyll

Glencoe & North Lorn Museum Association

Open mid-late May-Sep daily 10-5.30. Admission
charges.
L, <50%, G

12 miles south of Fort William off A82, parking for
cars, sales area, parties welcome but must book.

Two restored and thatched cottages, one of the
'cruck' type, contain MacDonald and Jacobite
relics, domestic bygones, weapons, embroidery
and costume. A recently extended building
gives more room to exhibit agricultural items.
Also a display on the Ballachulish slate
industry.

GOLSPIE

DUNROBIN CASTLE

Golspie, Sutherland KW10 6RP
Tel:(04083) 3177
Correspondence to Sutherland Estates Office, Duke
Street, Golspie KW10 6RP

Sutherland Trust

Open May Mon-Thur 10.30-12.30 Jun-Sep Mon-
Sat 10.30-5.30 Sun 1-5.30. Last admission 5. Groups
accepted outside open dates with 24 hours notice.
Museum open Jun-Sep 11-4.30. Admission charges
(with concessions).
ST, <50%, G

1/2 mile north of Golspie on A9, parking for cars &
coaches, refreshments, sales area, wc, parties welcome
no need to book.

The earliest part of the building dates from
1275 but large additions were made in 1680,
1780 and 1850. Now a spired, fairy-tale castle,
Dunrobin looks onto magnificent formal
gardens that link the castle to the sea. The
state rooms are open to the public and contain
collections of pictures, furniture, silver and
household objects. The Victorian museum in
the grounds has recently been restored and
contains a unique collection of Pictish stones
as well as big game trophies and local history,
ethnographic and archaeological items. Rail
excursions are run from Inverness to Dunrobin
station during the summer months.

HELMSDALE

TIMESPAN

Dunrobin Street, Helmsdale, Sutherland
Tel:(04312) 327

Helmsdale Heritage Society

Open Easter-mid Oct Mon-Sat 10-5 Sun 2-5.
Admission charges (with concessions).
P, R, 100%, WC, G, AD

In town on A9 North of Inverness, parking for cars
& coaches, refreshments, sales area, wc.

This award-winning visitor centre uses
audiovisual techniques to provide visitor-
activated sets telling the story of the people
of the Highlands. Other displays include the
natural history of the area. There is a riverside
garden of rare and medicinal plants.

INVERNESS

EDEN COURT GALLERY

Eden Court Theatre, Inverness IV3 5SA
Tel:(0463) 239841

Governors of Eden Court

Open all year Mon-Sat & selected Sun 10.30-10
(subject to occasional variation). Admission to gallery
free.
P, L/R/ST, WC, H, G, C, B

On riverside in town centre, parking for cars &
coaches, refreshments, sales area, temporary
exhibitions, wc, parties welcome (must book for
theatre).

The stalls and circle foyer of the theatre provide
gallery facilities for a regular programme of
small, monthly exhibitions by contemporary
artists.

INVERNESS MUSEUM & ART GALLERY

Castle Wynd, Inverness IV2 3ED
Tel:(0463) 237114

Inverness District Council

Open all year Mon-Sat 9-5. Admission free.
R, 50%, G, C

Town centre, refreshments, sales area, temporary
exhibitions, wc, parties welcome but must book.

The museum has new local history,
archaeology and wildlife displays. Local life
and industry are illustrated in reconstructions
of an Inverness cottage of the 1930's and
a taxidermist's workshop. There is also an
important display of Highland silver. The art
gallery has a full programme of temporary
exhibitions and events.

ISLE OF SKYE

CLAN DONALD CENTRE - MUSEUM OF THE ISLES

Armadale Castle, Sleat, Isle of Skye
Tel:(047 14) 305 / 227

Clan Donald Lands Trust

Open Apr-Oct daily 10-5.30. Last entry 5pm.
Admission charges (with concessions).
P, L, R, 100%, WC, G, C, B

1/4 mile from Armadale Pier off A851, parking for
cars & coaches, refreshments, sales area, wc, parties
welcome.

The Museum of the Isles is part of Skye's
award-winning Clan Donald Centre. Set in 40
acres of woodland gardens, the museum is
housed in the restored 18th century part of
Armadale Castle, once the home of Lord
Macdonald. An audio-visual presentation 'The
Sea Kingdom' and graphic displays tell the
story of 1300 years of Clan Donald history -
in particular the Lordship of the Isles, when
the Gaelic Nation flourished under the Clan's
leadership. During 1990 a new gallery
displaying artefacts relating to the Clan will
open, with a study area and temporary
exhibition space. There is a varied programme
of guided walks, Ranger service and arts events.

CNOC AN T-SITHEIN MUSEUM

Ellishadder, Staffin, Isle of Skye IV51 9JE

Dugald Ross

Open all year Mon-Sat 9-9. Admission charges.
P, L/R, 100%, G

15 miles north of Portree, parking for cars & coaches,
parties welcome no need to book.

A collection of local fossils is housed in this
small thatched museum. Contents also include
Bronze Age arrowheads and pottery, crofting
implements and 19th century furniture.

COLBOST FOLK MUSEUM

Colbost, Isle of Skye
Tel:(047 022) 296

Peter MacAskill

Open Easter-Oct daily 10-6. Other times by
appointment. Admission charges (with concessions).
ST, <50%, G

North west of Dunvegan off B884, parking for cars,
parties welcome no need to book.

This black house museum, furnished as a 19th
century croft house, contains folk life material.

12   The visitor centre in converted stables at the Clan Donald Centre, Isle of Skye. *[Pavel Satny]*

DUNVEGAN CASTLE

Dunvegan, Isle of Skye
Tel:(047022) 206

John MacLeod of MacLeod

Open Apr-Oct Mon-Sat 10-5.30. Other times by arrangement. Admission charges (with concessions). Gardens only open Sun.
P, L/ST, <50%, WC, G, C, B, AD

West coast of Skye on A863, parking for cars & coaches, refreshments, sales area, wc, parties welcome no need to book.

Home of the Chief of Macleod, this historic castle by the sea contains Clan Macleod and Celtic relics, including the Fairy Flag and Rory Mor's Horn. Gardens and pit dungeon are also open.

GIANT MACASKILL MUSEUM

Dunvegan, Isle of Skye
Tel:(047 022) 296

Peter MacAskill

Open Easter-Oct Mon-Sat 10-5.30 Sun 12.30-5. Other times by appointment. Admission charges (with concessions).
P, L, 100%, G

In town, parking for cars & coaches.

The displays tell stories of the feats of the 7'9" giant. There is a model of him and replicas of his chair, table and bed.

LUIB FOLK MUSEUM

Luib, Isle of Skye
Tel:(047 022) 296

Peter MacAskill

Open Easter-Oct daily 9-6. Other times by appointment. Admission chages (with concessions). ST, <50%, G

7 miles north west of Broadford on A850, parking for cars & coaches, parties welcome no need to book.

An atmospheric black house museum showing living conditions in Skye in the early 20th century.

THE PIPING HERITAGE CENTRE

Borreraig, Dunvegan, Isle of Skye
Tel:(047 081) 284

Hugh Ross MacCrimmon

Open Easter-late Oct Mon-Sat 10-6 Sun 2-6. Other times by appointment. Admission charges. 100%, G

Parking for cars, refreshments, sales area, wc, parties welcome but must book.

Exhibition shows how pipes are made and tells the stories and history of Pibroch, the MacCrimmons and other piping families. Photographs of pipes from other lands as well as examples from Scotland.

13   Master thatcher John Warner working on a clackmill at the Highland Folk Museum in Kingussie. School children are learning about building methods and materials. *[Highland Folk Museum]*

SKYE MUSEUM OF ISLAND LIFE

Kilmuir, Portree, Isle of Skye
Tel:(047 052) 279

Mr. J. MacDonald

Open Apr-Oct Mon-Sat 9-5.30. Admission charges. P, L, 50%, WC, G, C

2 miles south of Duntulm off A855, parking for cars & coaches, sales area, wc, parties welcome no need to book.

The crofting life in Skye is described in this museum. A weaver's house, an old smithy and a furnished black house make up just part of the display.

KINGUSSIE

HIGHLAND FOLK MUSEUM

Duke Street, Kingussie PH21 1JG
Tel:(0540) 661307

Highland Regional Council

Open all year Apr-Oct Mon-Sat 10-6 Sun 2-6 Nov-Mar Mon-Fri 10-3. Admission charges (with concessions).
R/ST, WC, G

39 miles south of Inverness off A9, parking for cars & coaches, sales area, temporary exhibitions, wc, parties welcome booking preferred.

The first folk museum to be established in Scotland (1934). Important collections contain excellent examples of Highland life with domestic, agricultural and industrial items. Open-air exhibits include a Lewis black house and a 'click' mill, a turf-built kailyard, agricultural equipment, old vehicles, wagons and carts. Traditional events (spinning, music, handcrafts) are held throughout the main summer season.

LATHERON

CLAN GUNN HERITAGE CENTRE & MUSEUM

Latheron, Caithness
Correspondence to Mrs Gunn, Latheronwheel, Latheron, Caithness.

Clan Gunn Heritage Trust

Open summer Mon-Sat 11-6. Admission charges.

South of Wick on A9, parking for cars & coaches, sales area, wc, parties welcome no need to book.

The history of Orkney and the North is blended with the story of the Clan Gunn and its Norse origins in this small museum.

14 Domestic and agricultural displays at the Nairn Literary Institute Museum, Nairn. *[Gordon Lyall]*

LYTH

LYTH ARTS CENTRE

Lyth, nr. Wick, Caithness
Tel:(095 584) 270

Lyth Arts Society

Open late Jun-early Sep daily 10-6. Admission charges (with concessions).
P, L/ST, 100%, G, C, B

10 miles north of Wick off A9, parking for cars, refreshments, sales area, temporary exhibitions, wc, parties welcome but must book.

This old village school, deep in the country, is the venue for varied exhibitions of contemporary painting, sculpture, photography and craft work. Musical and theatrical performances are held regularly throughout the season.

NAIRN

CAWDOR CASTLE

Nairn, Inverness-shire IV12 5RD
Tel:(066 77) 615

Earl of Cawdor

Open May-early Oct daily 10-5.30. Last admission 5. Admission charges (with concessions).
P, R, <50%, WC, G, C, B

5 miles south west of Nairn on B9090, parking for cars & coaches, refreshments, sales area, temporary exhibitions, wc, parties welcome booking preferred.

This 14th century tower house with considerable 17th century additions contains an interesting array of Victoriana including a Royal Mail tricycle c.1860. The castle is used as a private residence and is comfortably furnished with some fine antiques and paintings. Splendid gardens are also open to the public.

NAIRN FISHERTOWN MUSEUM

Laing Hall, King Street, Nairn
Tel:(0667) 52064
Correspondence to Secretary, B. Mein, 37 Park Street, Nairn.

Nairn Fishertown Museum Committee

Open Jun-Sep Mon,Wed,Fri 2.30-4.30 & 6.30-8.30 Tue,Thu,Sat 2.30-4.30. Admission charges.
P, L, G

Near harbour, parking for cars & coaches nearby, wc, parties welcome but must book.

A collection of photographs and items concerning the domestic life of the fishertown and the fishing industry around the Moray Firth.

NAIRN LITERARY INSTITUTE MUSEUM

Viewfield House, Nairn

Literary Institute

Open Mon-Sat 2.30-4.30. Admission free.
ST

Town centre, parking for cars & coaches, wc, parties welcome but must book.

The Institute's collections date back almost 150 years, but are housed in premises renovated for the purpose in 1985. A shrunken head from Ecuador, exquisitely coloured Northern Plains Indian leggings and moccasins are amongst the wide-ranging ethnographic collection. Iron pots, butter churns and crofting tools are some of the objects on display in the folk life gallery. Rocks, minerals, fossils and natural history are also represented.

NEWTONMORE

CLAN MACPHERSON HOUSE & MUSEUM

Main Street, Newtonmore, Inverness
Tel:(054 03) 332
Correspondence to Hon. Secretary, John Macpherson Martin, 81 Runneymede, Merton Abbey, London SW19 2PG.

Clan Macpherson Trust

Open May-Sep Mon-Sat 10-5.30 Sun 2.30-5.30. Other times by arrangement. Admission free.
P, R, 100%, G

Village centre, parking for cars, sales area, parties welcome no need to book.

This museum tells the story of the Clan Macpherson and related families. Relics associated with Prince Charles Edward Stuart (Bonnie Prince Charlie) are also on display.

ROSEMARKIE

GROAM HOUSE MUSEUM

High Street, Rosemarkie, Ross-shire
Tel:(0381) 20924

Fortrose & Rosemarkie Community Council

Open May-Sep Mon-Sat 11-5 Sun 2.30-4.30. Admission charges.
L, 100%, G, AD

Centre of Rosemarkie north of Inverness on A832, parking for cars & coaches, sales area, parties welcome but must book.

A Pictish Centre with carved Pictish symbol stones, hangings and reproductions of all the Pictish stones in Ross & Cromarty. Video films and a photographic archive available. Access outside summer season by arrangement.

SPITTAL

FOSSIL VISITORS CENTRE

Spittal Village Hall, Spittal, Caithness
Correspondence to Mr K MacLennan, Knockglass Cottage, Watten, Caithness

Spittal Village Hall Committee and Spittal Action Centre

Open Jun-Sep daily 10-4. Other times by arrangement. Admission charges.
P, L, 50%, G, C

8 miles from Thurso, on A895 Latheron to Georgemas Road, parking for cars & coaches, refreshments, sales area, wc.

This area, on the edge of the Flow country of Caithness, was once the centre of a thriving flagstone cutting industry. Exhibitions in part of the village hall tell the story of the Spittal Flagstone Quarries and the fossils found in the stone.

STRATHPEFFER

STRATHPEFFER SPA EXHIBITION

The Pump Room, The Square, Strathpeffer, Ross-shire IV14 9AS
Tel:(0997) 21214

Norscot/Victorian Strathpeffer Committee

Open May-Sep daily 10-12 & 2.30-4.30. Admission charges.
P, L, 100%, G

Town centre, parking for cars & coaches, parties welcome no need to book.

Display of old photographs of Victorian Strathpeffer, situated in the former Pump Room building.

TAIN

TAIN MUSEUM & CLAN ROSS CENTRE

Castle Brae, Tain, Ross-shire IV19 1AJ
Tel:(0862) 2140

Tain & District Museum Trust

Open Easter-Sep Mon-Sat 10-4.30. Other times by arrangement. Admission charges (with concessions).
PPA, ST, AD

Off main street, parking for cars & coaches nearby, sales area, parties welcome but must book.

This small museum houses the Clan Ross Centre, and holds collections of Tain silver, 17th century silver coins from Ardross, historic documents and photographs relating to the area.

THURSO

THURSO HERITAGE MUSEUM

Town Hall, High Street, Thurso KW14 8AG
Correspondence to Mrs. Corner, Morven, Olrig St, Thurso.

Thurso Heritage Society

Open Jun-Sep Mon-Sat 10-1 & 2-5. Admission charges.
P, ST, 50%, G

Town centre, parking nearby, sales area, not suitable for large parties.

Displays in this local history museum include fossils, carved stones, the flagstone industry of Caithness, and an exhibition of photographs of Thurso before and after the coming of Dounreay Power Station. There are also sections on Sir John Sinclair, author of the first Statistical Account of Scotland and Robert Dick, the Victorian botanist and geologist.

ULLAPOOL

LOCHBROOM HIGHLAND MUSEUM

Quay Street, Ullapool IV26 2UE
Tel:(0463) 2356

Lochbroom Community Association

Open Apr-Sep Mon-Sat 9-5. Admission free.
L, G, C, B

Town centre, not suitable for large parties.

A small idiosyncratic museum at the back of a bookshop with displays relating to Wester Ross (military, agricultural, social, geological and natural history).

WICK

WICK HERITAGE CENTRE

Bank Row, Wick, Caithness KW1 5EY

Wick Heritage Society

Open Jun-Sep Mon-Sat 10-12 & 2-5. Admission charges (with concessions).
PPA, ST

Town centre, sales area, wc, parties welcome but must book.

A fish kiln and a working lighthouse are amongst the displays at this local history museum which specialises in the sea and the herring industry. The museum also houses the Johnston collection of 70,000 photographs taken in Caithness and dating from the 1860's. A terraced garden behind the museum offers scenic views of the town.

15   Bronze messenger figures in cast bronze, made in Benin in the 17th and 18th century. In the collections of the Royal Museum of Scotland, Edinburgh.

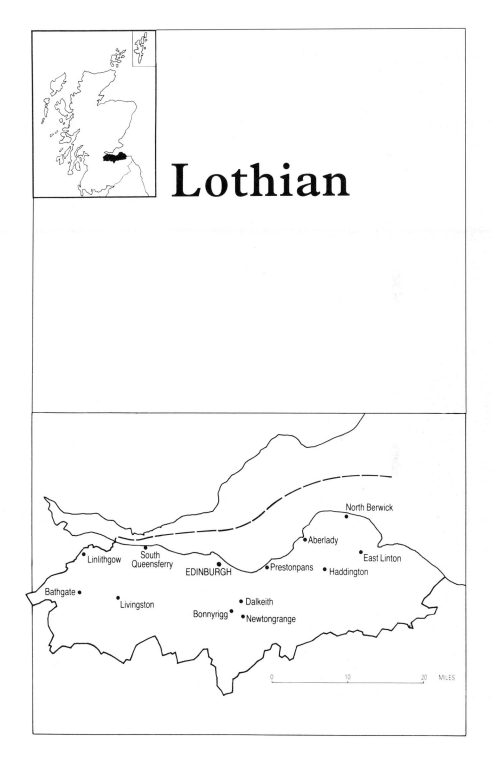

Lothian

ABERLADY

MYRETON MOTOR MUSEUM

Aberlady, East Lothian
Tel:(087 57) 288

Private

Open daily May-Sep 10-6 Oct-Apr 10-5. Admission charges.
P, L, 50%, WC, G

17 miles east of Edinburgh off A198, parking for cars & coaches, sales area, temporary exhibitions, wc, parties welcome but must book.

Cars from 1897, motor-cycles from 1903, commercial vehicles from 1919, cycles from 1866, Second World War British military vehicles and aero-engines are just part of the ever-increasing collection of vehicles at this museum. Motoring accessories, posters and signs also on display. A museum quiz book is available for children.

BATHGATE

BENNIE MUSEUM

9-11 Mansefield Street, Bathgate, West Lothian EH48 4HU
Tel:(0506) 634944

Bathgate Community Council

Open all year Mon-Sat 10-4.30. Admission free.
PPA, L/ST, 100%, G

Town centre, parking nearby, wc, parties welcome but must book.

Two joined cottages, the earliest part dating from the 18th century, house this local museum. Dr Simpson, inventor of chloroform, and 'Paraffin' Young, both of Bathgate, are represented in displays. The collection includes fine early photographs, glass from the extinct Bathgate glassworks and Victoriana.

BONNYRIGG

LASSWADE HIGH SCHOOL CENTRE

Eskdale Drive, Bonnyrigg, Midlothian EH19 2LA
Tel:(031) 663 7171

Lothian Regional Council

Open during school terms Mon-Thu 8am-9pm Fri 8-5. Admission free.
P, L/R, 100%, WC, G, C

In Bonnyrigg 8 miles from Edinburgh city centre, parking for cars & coaches, refreshments, sales area, temporary exhibitions, wc, parties welcome no need to book.

A small exhibition area within a community centre showing both local and touring exhibitions.

DALKEITH

DALKEITH ARTS CENTRE

White Hart Street, Dalkeith, Midlothian
Tel:(031) 663 6986
Correspondence to Dept. of Recreation & Leisure, 2 Clerk Street, Loanhead, Midlothian.

Midlothian District Council

Open all year Wed-Fri 10-12 & 2-4 Sat 10-12 (later for performances). Admission to exhibitions free.
L, R, 100%, WC, G, C

Town centre, parking for cars & coaches, refreshments, temporary exhibitions, wc, parties welcome no need to book.

The centre provides a varied and stimulating programme of exhibitions and musical events, mainly under the aegis of the Dalkeith Arts Guild.

EAST LINTON

PRESTON MILL & PHANTASSIE DOOCOT

East Linton, East Lothian
Tel:(0620) 860426

National Trust for Scotland

Open Apr-Sep Mon-Sat 11-1 & 2-5 Sun 2-5 Oct Sat 11-1 & 2-4 Sun 2-4. Admission charges (with concessions).
P, L/ST, 50%, G

23 miles east of Edinburgh off A1, parking for cars & coaches, temporary exhibitions, parties welcome but must book.

This 16th century mill is the oldest, mechanically working water-driven, meal mill in Scotland and was last commercially in production in 1957. The conical-roofed kiln, red pantiles and grouping of the buildings are popular with artists. The exhibition room shows the work of local craftsmen and painters. The Phantassie Doocot, a short walk away, once held 500 birds.

EDINBURGH

BANK OF SCOTLAND MUSEUM

Head Office, Bank of Scotland, The Mound, Edinburgh
Tel:(031) 243 5467

The Governors and Company of the Bank of Scotland

Open Jul-mid Sep Mon-Fri 9-4.45. Other times by appointment. Admission free.
ST, WC, G

City centre at The Mound, wc.

This museum tells the history of the Bank of Scotland and its associates, and of money in Scotland. The coin collection includes pre-1707 Scottish coins and post-1707 items from throughout the UK. There is a fascinating banknote collection and memorabilia from the history of the Bank.

CAMERA OBSCURA

Outlook Tower, Castlehill, Edinburgh EH1 2LZ
Tel:(031) 226 3709

Visitor Centres Ltd.

Open all year daily Nov-Mar 10-5 Apr-Oct 9.30-6. Admission charges (with concessions).
ST, G

At top of Royal Mile close to Castle, parking nearby, sales area, temporary exhibitions, parties welcome but must book.

Installed in 1850 on top of the Outlook Tower high above Edinburgh's historic Old Town, the Camera Obscura projects a live moving picture of the city onto a viewing table inside a darkened room. In addition there are exhibitions of holography, pin-hole photography and old Edinburgh in paintings and photographs.

CITY ART CENTRE

1-4 Market Street, Edinburgh
Tel:(031) 225 2424 ex.6650

Edinburgh District Council

Open all year Mon-Sat 10-5 Jun-Sep 10-6. Closed September 1990 to May 1992 for work on new extension. Admission free.
PPA, L, 100%, WC, G, C, B

City centre behind Waverley Station, refreshments, sales area, temporary exhibitions, wc, parties welcome but must book.

Opened in 1980, this gallery accommodates major temporary fine and decorative art exhibitions. The main strengths of the permanent collection are in works by late 19th and 20th century Scottish artists and topographical views. The 'Open Space' is available for community derived exhibitions.

COCKBURN MUSEUM

Department of Geology, King's Buildings, West Mains Road, Edinburgh EH9 3JF
Tel:(031) 667 1081 ex.3577

University of Edinburgh

Open all year Mon-Fri 9-5. Admission free.
P, R/ST, 100%, G

South side of Edinburgh, parking for cars & coaches, sales area, temporary exhibitions, wc, parties welcome but must book.

A small departmental museum geared to undergraduate teaching but with many displays of interest to the general public, including Mount St. Helen's Volcano, recent fossil finds and economic geology. Large collections of rocks, fossils, minerals, thin sections etc. (c.50,000 specimens) available for browsing or more intense study. Historical and teaching material available.

EDINBURGH CASTLE

Edinburgh
Tel:(031) 244 3101 for information.

Scottish Development Department (Historic Buildings and Monuments)

Open 4 Jan-Mar & Oct-Dec Mon-Sat 9.30-5 Sun 12.30-4.10 Apr-Sep Mon-Sat 9.30-5.50 Sun 11-5.50. Last admission 45 minutes before closing. Admission charges (with concessions).
PPA, R, WC, G, AD

City centre, parking nearby, sales area, wc, parties welcome.

This most famous Scottish castle, built on a massive basalt rock, has a complex building history. The Great Hall was built by James IV and the Half Moon Battery by the Regent Morton in the late 16th century. The crown jewels are displayed in the Royal apartments and Mons Meg, the famous 15th century gun can also be seen. Scotland's national shrine within the precincts of the castle contains the rolls of honour of all Scots men and women who died in the First and Second World Wars. See also The Royal Scots Regimental Museum and Scottish United Services Museum.

EDINBURGH COLLEGE OF ART SCULPTURE COURT & ANDREW GRANT GALLERY

Lauriston Place, Edinburgh EH3 9DF
Tel:(031) 229 9311

Governors of Edinburgh College of Art

Open during term times & Edinburgh Festival Mon-Thu 10-8.30 Fri 10-5 Sat 10-12. Admission free.
PPA, L/R/ST, 100%, WC, G

Near city centre, parking nearby, temporary exhibitions, wc, parties welcome no need to book.

The large Sculpture Court, the Andrew Grant Gallery and the Humanities Teaching Gallery provide a varied programme of exhibitions ranging from contemporary art and diploma shows to Afghanistan rugs. Occasional evening events are held.

EDINBURGH PRINTMAKERS

Wash-house, 23 Union Street, Edinburgh EH1 3LR
Tel:(031) 557 2479

Independent

Open all year Mon-Sat 10-6. During Edinburgh Festival also Sun 2-5. Admission free.
ST, <50%, G

Opposite Playhouse Theatre at east of city centre, sales area, temporary exhibitions, wc, parties welcome but must book.

Edinburgh Printmakers presents a versatile programme of exhibitions in its gallery. A viewing window in the gallery overlooks the workshop which has facilities for etching, lithography, screenprinting and photography. A selection of over 500 contemporary original prints by members are displayed in the sales area on the ground floor. Also on display are a selection of original prints by some of Scotland's major artists such as John Bellamy, Stephen Conroy, Barbara Rae, Elizabeth Blackadder and Peter Howson. The workshop also runs evening and weekend courses in screenprinting, lithography and etching.

EDINBURGH SCOUT MUSEUM

Edinburgh Scout Centre, 7 Valleyfield Street, Edinburgh EH3 9LP
Tel:(031) 229 3756

Edinburgh Area Scout Council

Open all year Mon-Fri 9.30-4.30. Admission free.
PPA, L/ST, 100%, WC, G

Tollcross near King's Theatre, not suitable for large groups.

A must for all Scouts past and present. Over 75 years of Scouting in Edinburgh and abroad are illustrated in this specialist museum.

EDINBURGH UNIVERSITY COLLECTION OF HISTORIC MUSICAL INSTRUMENTS

Reid Concert Hall, Bristo Square, Edinburgh EH8 9AG
Tel:(031) 667 1011 ex.2573 or (031) 447 4791

University of Edinburgh

Open all year Wed 3-5 Sat 10-1. During Edinburgh Festival also open Mon-Fri 2-5. Admission free.
PPA, ST, 100%, G

South side of city, sales area, temporary exhibitions, wc, parties welcome but must book.

One thousand musical instruments and related items on display including stringed and woodwind instruments, bagpipes, brass, percussion and ethnic instruments. The histories of the orchestra, wind band, brass band, parlour and popular music are illustrated. The museum houses the gift of the Macaulay Collection of 51 instruments of great importance.

FRENCH INSTITUTE

13 Randolph Crescent, Edinburgh EH3 7TT
Tel:(031) 225 5366

French Institute

Open all year Mon-Fri 9.30-5.30. Admission free.
ST, <50%, G

West end of city centre, parking nearby, cafe, temporary exhibitions, wc, parties welcome no need to book.

The French Institute has a small gallery in which it runs a yearly programme of exhibitions. Many are by contemporary French and Scottish artists.

FRUITMARKET GALLERY

29 Market Street, Edinburgh EH1 1DF
Tel:(031) 225 2383

Board of Directors

Open all year Tue,Wed,Fri,Sat 10-5.30 Thu 10-7 Sun 12-5.30. During Edinburgh Festival open daily Mon-Sat 10-7 Sun 2-5. Admission free.
L, 50%, G

City centre behind Waverley Station, refreshments, sales area, temporary exhibitions, wc, parties welcome no need to book.

Contemporary gallery with an impressive exhibition programme of painting, sculpture, prints and photography from the international art world. Special arrangements can be made for group visits.

Tam Docherty in his room at the Grove Street Model Lodging House, during the 1970s. One of a series of reconstructed scenes from everyday life at The People's Story, Edinburgh. [*City of Edinburgh Museums and Art Galleries*]

'An American Girl' by Gerald Laing, part of the permanent collection at Inverness Museum and Art Gallery. [*Scottish Museums Council*]

A friendly word from a warder in the Main Hall of the Royal Museum of Scotland, Edinburgh.
[*Royal Museum of Scotland, Edinburgh*]

THE GEORGIAN HOUSE

7 Charlotte Square, Edinburgh
Tel:(031) 225 2160

National Trust for Scotland

Open Apr-Oct Mon-Sat 10-5 Sun 2-5. Last admission 4.30. Admission charges (with concessions).
ST, <50%, H, G, AD

West end of city centre, sales area, parties welcome but must book.

Furnished as an elegant New Town house of the late 18th century with contents covering the period 1760-1820. Admission includes an audio-visual programme on Georgian Edinburgh.

GLADSTONE'S LAND

447b Lawnmarket, Edinburgh
Tel:(031) 226 5856

National Trust for Scotland

Open Apr-Oct Mon-Sat 10-5 Sun 2-5. Last admission 4.30. Admission charges (with concessions).
ST, <50%, G

City centre in Royal Mile, sales area, parties welcome but must book.

A six-storey 17th century tenement with one floor furnished as the home of a merchant of the period and the ground floor reconstructed as a 17th century shop front with a cloth merchant's booth. Of special interest is a remarkable painted ceiling of 1620. The Gladstone Gallery on the 2nd floor features changing exhibitions by contemporary artists.

HOLYROOD PARK VISITOR CENTRE

Holyrood Lodge, 140 Holyrood Road, Edinburgh EH8 8AX
Tel:(031) 556 7561
Correspondence to Scottish Wildlife Trust, 25 Johnston Terrace, Edinburgh EH1 2NH.

Scottish Wildlife Trust

Open Jun-Sep daily 12-4 Apr-May & Oct-Dec Sat,Sun only 10-4. Closed during Queen's residence. Admission free.
L, 100%, G

Opposite south entrance to Palace of Holyrood House, parking nearby, sales area, not suitable for large parties.

A permanent exhibition on the history, geology and wildlife of the Royal Park of Holyrood, illustrated with photographic displays and a 3-dimensional geological model.

HUNTLY HOUSE MUSEUM

142 Canongate, Edinburgh
Tel:(031) 225 2424 ex.6689

Edinburgh District Council

Open all year Mon-Sat 10-5 Jun-Sep 10-6. Admission free.
ST, <50%, G

City centre in Royal Mile, sales area, temporary exhibitions, wc, parties welcome but must book.

Edinburgh's principal museum of local history is housed in a fine example of a restored 16th century town mansion. It contains important collections of Edinburgh silver and glass, Scottish pottery, shop-signs and relics concerning Field Marshal Earl Haig. Imaginative reconstructions show the city's traditional industries and domestic life of the past.

JOHN KNOX HOUSE

45 High Street, Edinburgh EH1 1SR
Tel:(031) 556 9579 or 2647

Church of Scotland

Open Mon-Sat 10-4.30. Admission charges (with concessions).
<50%, H, G

City centre in Royal Mile, sales area, parties welcome but must book.

This picturesque 15th century town house is associated both with John Knox the Scottish Church reformer, and James Mossman the goldsmith who was keeper of the Royal Mint to Mary, Queen of Scots. Guided tours and a puzzle trail for children are available.

LADY STAIR'S HOUSE

Lady Stair's Close, Lawnmarket, Edinburgh
Tel:(031) 225 2424 ex.6593
Correspondence to City Curator, Huntly House, 142 Canongate, Edinburgh EH8 8DD.

Edinburgh District Council

Open all year Mon-Sat 10-5 Jun-Sep 10-6. Admission free.
ST, <50%

City centre in Royal Mile, sales area, parties welcome but must book.

This town house, built in 1622 and named after its 18th century owner Elizabeth, the Dowager Countess of Stair, now contains portraits, relics and manuscripts of three of Scotland's greatest men of letters - Robert Burns, Sir Walter Scott and Robert Louis Stevenson.

LATE VICTORIAN PHARMACY

36 York Place, Edinburgh EH1 3HU
Tel:(031) 556 4386

Royal Pharmaceutical Society of Great Britain

Open all year Mon-Fri 9-5. Admission free.
ST, G

East end of city centre, not suitable for large parties (max 12).

A unique collection of historic pharmaceutical material displayed in a shop setting.

LAURISTON CASTLE

Cramond Road South, Edinburgh
Tel:(031) 336 2060 or 1912

Edinburgh District Council

Open Apr-Oct Sat-Thu 10-1 & 2-5 Nov-Mar Sat & Sun only 2-4. Admission charges (with concessions).
PPA, ST, <50%

5 miles west of city centre, parking for cars, sales area, wc, parties welcome but must book.

This late 16th century tower house with 19th century Jacobean style additions was left to the nation in 1926 on condition that the furnishings would not be changed. The important Edwardian interior is still intact and contains period and reproduction furniture, an impressive collection of Derbyshire Blue John ornaments, a unique collection of Crossley Wool mosaics and a wide range of other 'objets d'art'. Party bookings can be made to the Custodian, Lauriston Castle.

MALTINGS INTERPRETATION CENTRE

Cramond Village, Edinburgh
Correspondence to The Secretary, 90 Whitehouse Road, Edinburgh EH4 6PD.

Cramond Heritage Trust

Open Jun-Sep Sat,Sun 2.30-5. Admission free.
Cramond Village on harbour front, parking nearby, sales area, temporary exhibitions, wc, parties welcome but must book.

The main exhibition shows the history of Cramond village from Roman times to the present day. Guided walks organised by the Cramond Heritage Society held every Sunday at 3.15pm from June to September (meet at the Kirkgate). Guides describe the story of the Roman fort, medieval Bishop's tower, kirk yard, 17th century Cramond house, village and harbour.

MUSEUM OF CHILDHOOD

42 High Street, Edinburgh
Tel:(031) 225 2424 ex.6647

Edinburgh District Council

Open all year Mon-Sat 10-5 Jun-Sep 10-6. Admission free.
L, 50%, WC, G

City centre in Royal Mile, sales area, wc, parties welcome but must book.

This museum is the first museum in the world devoted solely to the history of childhood. It contains collections of historic toys as well as displays relating to the clothing, health, education and upbringing of children past and present. When in full swing it is also said to be the noisiest museum in the world!

MUSEUM OF COMMUNICATION

James Clerk Maxwell Building, University of Edinburgh, Mayfield Road, Edinburgh EH9 3JL
Correspondence to C.H.C. Matthews, 22 Kinglass Avenue, Bo'ness, West Lothian EH51 9QA.
Tel:(0506) 823507.

C.H.C. Matthews

Open all year Mon-Sat 9-9 Sun 9-7. Admission free.
P, R/ST, 100%, WC, G, SL

At Kings Buildings, Liberton, parking for cars, wc, parties welcome booking preferred (max 20).

The collection outlines the history of electrical communication and includes spark transmitters from the First World War, crystal receivers, early valves and valve receivers. It also contains examples of teleprinters and television receivers, 'spy-sets' and distress senders for marine and aircraft use. Radio and talking books available for the blind. Braille and Moon raised script also on show.

MUSEUM OF FIRE

Lothian and Borders Fire Brigade, Lauriston Place, Edinburgh
Tel:(031) 228 2401

Lothian & Borders Joint Fire Board

Open by appointment daily 9-1 & 2-4. Admission free.
PPA, L, 100%, WC, G

Near city centre, parties welcome but must book.

A must for all would-be firemen this museum, housed in a former fire station, contains a fascinating collection of objects relating to fire brigades and fire fighting from 1600 to the present day.

MUSEUM OF LIGHTING

59 St. Stephen Street, Edinburgh EH3 5AH
Tel:(031) 556 4503

W.M. Purves

Open all year Sat 1-6. Other times by appointment. Admission free.
L

City centre 1/2 mile north of Princes Street, parking nearby, sales area, wc, not suitable for large parties.

This small private museum is housed in a restored Georgian shop and contains an interesting collection of oil, gas and electrical domestic and transport lighting of the 19th and early 20th centuries.

NATIONAL GALLERY OF SCOTLAND

The Mound, Edinburgh EH2 2EL
Tel:(031) 556 8921

Trustees of the National Galleries of Scotland

Open all year Mon-Sat 10-5 Sun 2-5. Hours extended during Edinburgh Festival. Admission free.
R, 100%, WC

City centre off Princes Street, sales area, temporary exhibitions, wc, parties welcome booking preferred.

Housed in an elegant neo-classical building by William Playfair, this fine collection of paintings includes works by Constable, El Greco, Rembrandt, Monet and Vermeer - a host of masterpieces from about 1400-1900. Scottish painting is superbly represented and includes works by Raeburn, Ramsay, Wilkie and MacTaggart. The gallery also contains a collection of some 19,000 prints, watercolours and drawings including the famous Vaughan Bequest of Turner watercolours shown every January. Regular temporary exhibitions and lunchtime lectures and occasional concerts are held. The education department for the National Galleries provides workshops, projects etc. for schools.

NATIONAL LIBRARY OF SCOTLAND

George IV Bridge, Edinburgh EH1 1EW
Tel:(031) 226 4531

Trustees of the National Library of Scotland

Open all year. Exhibition room Mon-Fri 9.30-5 Sat 9.30-1 Sun 2-5. Reading rooms Mon-Fri 9.30-8.30 Sat 9.30-1. Admission free.
L, 100%, WC, G

City centre near Royal Mile, sales area, temporary exhibitions, wc.

Exhibitions ranging from Scottish history to modern calligraphy and including figures as diverse as Mary Queen of Scots, Andrew Carnegie, Robert Burns and David Livingstone, are shown throughout the year. Most are drawn from the Library's rich collections of printed books and manuscripts from the Middle Ages to the present day, but loan exhibitions, sometimes from abroad, are also shown.

PALACE OF HOLYROOD HOUSE & HOLYROOD ABBEY

Edinburgh
Tel:(031) 556 1096

Royal Palaces Presentation Office

Open summer Mon-Sat 9.30-5.15 Sun 10.30-4.30 Winter Mon-Sat 9.30-3.45. Admission charges (with concessions).
L, 50%, G

At east end of the Royal Mile, parking for cars & coaches nearby, parties welcome.

The oldest part of the Palace is the north west tower, built by James V and used by Mary Queen of Scots. The rest of the building was reconstructed by Sir William Bruce for Charles II in 1671-79. Now the official residence of The Queen in Scotland, the Palace contains state apartments with tapestries, furniture and paintings from the 16th-19th centuries, including a portrait gallery with paintings of over 100 Scottish sovereigns. The ruined nave of the 12th and 13th century abbey church, built for Augustinian canons, is adjacent.

RIAS GALLERY

15 Rutland Square, Edinburgh EH1 2BE
Tel:(031) 229 7545

Royal Incorporation of Architects in Scotland

Open all year Mon-Fri 9.30-5. Admission free.
ST, 50%, G

West end of city centre, parking nearby, sales area, temporary exhibitions, wc, parties welcome but must book.

The house at 15 Rutland Square was gifted to the Royal Incorporation of Architects in Scotland by its founder, Sir Robert Rowand Anderson. The gallery mounts high quality exhibitions relating to the built environment and the work of architects in particular. The library can be visited by appointment.

RICHARD DEMARCO GALLERY

17-21 Blackfriars Street, Edinburgh EH1 1NB
Tel:(031) 557 0707

Board of Directors

Open all year Mon-Sat 10-6.30. Admission free.
PPA, L, <50%, G

City centre near Royal Mile, sales area, temporary exhibitions, wc, parties welcome but must book.

The Demarco Gallery has been a feature of the contemporary art world for over 20 years. A changing programme of international exhibitions of 20th century art is organised by the gallery.

THE ROYAL COLLEGE OF SURGEONS OF EDINBURGH MUSEUM & HISTORICAL MUSEUM

Nicholson Street, Edinburgh EH8 9DW
Tel:(031) 556 6206

Council of the Royal College of Surgeons of Edinburgh

College museum open all year (closed on approx 60 days when used for educational purposes) by appointment, Historical Museum open all year by appointment. Admission free.
PPA, ST, 50%, WC, G

City centre, temporary exhibitions, parties welcome but must book.

The College Museum consists of one of the largest and most comprehensive collections of surgical pathological specimens in this country, together with instruments and illustrations. The Historical Museum illustrates the history of surgery and of the college over nearly 500 years and includes items from the College's collection. The museum also tells the story of some of Edinburgh's famous surgeons and anatomists and of their professional organisation, the Royal College of Surgeons of Edinburgh. It houses the famous Menzies Campbell Historical Dental Collection. Disabled access to the pathological museum only.

ROYAL MUSEUM OF SCOTLAND

Chambers Street, Edinburgh EH1 1JF
Tel:(031) 225 7534

Trustees of the National Museums of Scotland

Open all year Mon-Sat 10-5 Sun 2-5. Admission free.
L/ST, 100%, WC, H, G, C

City centre near Royal Mile, parking nearby, refreshments, sales area, temporary exhibitions, wc, parties welcome but must book.

The national collections of decorative arts of the world, ethnography, natural sciences, technology and science housed in one building. This comprehensive collection includes European and Oriental ceramics and metal work, Egyptology, arms and armour and primitive art. There are international natural history rooms and an important collection of fossils and minerals. The Evolution Wing tells the story of life from its beginning. Technology displays include 'Wylam Dilly', one of the oldest locomotives in existence, an industrial waterwheel, various ship models, push-button model steam engines and a collection of scientific instruments of international renown. The education department provides an active programme for children and adults including lectures, concerts, films, competitions, workshops and other related activities.

ROYAL MUSEUM OF SCOTLAND

Queen Street, Edinburgh EH2 1JD
Tel:(031) 225 7534

Trustees of the National Museums of Scotland

Open all year Mon-Sat 10-5 Sun 2-5. Admission free.
R/ST, 100%, WC, G

East end of city centre, sales area, wc, parties welcome but must book.

Sharing premises with the National Portrait Gallery, this part of the Royal Museum houses Scottish material from prehistoric times to the present day. The archaeological collections contain some of the most important material in the U.K. Displays include objects from medieval to modern times telling the rich cultural story of Scotland. See Royal Museum of Scotland, Chambers Street for details of educational activities.

ROYAL OBSERVATORY VISITOR CENTRE

Blackford Hill, Edinburgh
Tel:(031) 668 8100 or 8405

Science & Engineering Research Council

Open all year Mon-Fri 10-4 Sat,Sun & public holidays 12-5. Other times by appointment. Admission charges (with concessions).
PPA, L, 50%, WC, G

3 miles south of city centre, parking for cars & coaches, sales area, temporary exhibitions, wc, parties welcome but must book.

Built on Blackford Hill and surrounded by open parkland, the Observatory has panoramic views of the city. The Visitor Centre is housed in the original 1894 building and has permanent exhibitions describing the history and current work of the Royal Observatory here and abroad. Temporary exhibitions include

16 Ceremonial Tabard of an Officer of Arms, 18th century. Made from silk appliquèd and embroidered with metal threads and glass beads. From the collections of the Royal Museum of Scotland, Edinburgh

17 Pieces from Bonnie Prince Charlie's silver travelling canteen made in Edinburgh in 1740–41 by Ebenezar Oliphant, a Jacobite silversmith. Now in the collections of the Royal Museum of Scotland.

sections on current space research and are illustrated with photographs from space probes. Displays include computer simulations and videos. The two large domes which house a 0.9m reflecting telescope and a Schmidt telescope are included in the tour and a 'Popular Observatory' allows the public to observe the night sky under professional supervision. An excellent educational facility, the centre provides lectures, films, talks and projects for schools and societies.

ROYAL SCOTS MUSEUM

The Castle, Edinburgh EH1 2YT
Tel:(031) 336 1761 ex.4265

Royal Scots Regimental Museum

Open May-Sep Mon-Sat 9.30-4.30 Sun 11-4.30 Oct-Apr Mon-Fri 9.30-4.OO. Admission free but charge for Castle.
PPA, L, 100%, G, C

City centre, limited parking, sales area, temporary exhibitions, parties welcome no need to book.

Regimental relics including uniforms, medals, colours, banners and paintings of the Royal Scots, the oldest regular regiment of infantry in the British Army and one of the most ancient in the world.

ROYAL SCOTTISH ACADEMY

The Mound, Princes Street, Edinburgh EH2 2EL
Tel:(031) 225 6671

The Royal Scottish Academy

Open end Apr-end Jul Mon-Sat 10-6 Sun 2-5. See press for details at other times of year. Admission charges (with concessions).
PPA, R/ST, 50%, WC, G

City centre, sales area, temporary exhibitions, wc, parties welcome but must book.

Works by contemporary Scottish artists predominate in the regular exhibitions held in this imposing Playfair building. Major international exhibitions often held during the Edinburgh Festival.

RUSSELL COLLECTION OF EARLY KEYBOARD INSTRUMENTS

St. Cecilia's Hall, Niddry Street, Cowgate, Edinburgh EH1 1LJ
Tel:(031) 667 1011 ex.4415

University of Edinburgh

Open all year Wed & Sat 2-5. During Edinburgh Festival Mon-Sat 10.30-12.30. Admission charges (with concessions).
ST, 100%, G

City centre, sales area, wc, parties welcome but must book.

An important collection of early keyboard instruments including clavichords, chamber organs and early pianos housed in a restored Georgian concert hall, built in 1762 by Robert Mylne to a unique oval plan. Paintings, textiles and tapestries are also exhibited. Musical events are held throughout the year.

SCOTTISH AGRICULTURAL MUSEUM

Ingliston, Edinburgh
Correspondence to Royal Museum of Scotland, Chambers Street, Edinburgh EH1 1JF. Tel:(031) 225 7534.

Trustees of the National Museums of Scotland

Open 16 Apr-Sep Mon-Fri 10-6.30. Admission free.
P, ST, 100%, WC, G

Off A8 (turn off at Edinburgh Airport), parking for cars & coaches, sales area, wc, parties welcome no need to book.

Part of the National Museums of Scotland, this museum concentrates on the social history of the Scottish countryside and contains fascinating displays covering all aspects of rural life. See Royal Museum of Scotland, Chambers Street for details of educational activities.

SCOTTISH NATIONAL GALLERY OF MODERN ART

Belford Road, Edinburgh EH4 3DR
Tel:(031) 556 8921

Trustees of the National Galleries of Scotland

Open all year Mon-Sat 10-5 Sun 2-5. Admission free.
P, R, 100%, WC, C

Near west end of city centre, parking for cars & coaches, refreshments, sales area, temporary exhibitions, wc, parties welcome booking preferred.

Recently moved to a large neo-classical building designed by William Burn in 1825, this collection of modern art is the most comprehensive of its kind in Britain outside the Tate in London. Built up over a relatively short period the collection, founded in 1960, includes works by the major artists representing the main movements of 20th century art. Cubists Braque and Picasso, expressionists Kirchner and Nolde, surrealist works by Ernst and Magritte and pop art by Lichtenstein and Hockney are just a few. The Scottish collection includes work by Caddell,

18 The construction of stringed instruments. A display at the Edinburgh University Collection of Historic Musical Instruments.

19 Henry Moore's 'Reclining Figure' in the grounds of the Scottish National Gallery of Modern Art, Edinburgh.

Fergusson, Eardley, Gillies and Redpath. Sculptures are sited in the wooded grounds. See National Gallery of Scotland for details of educational activities.

SCOTTISH NATIONAL PORTRAIT GALLERY

1 Queen Street, Edinburgh EH2 1JD
Tel:(031) 556 8921

Trustees of the National Galleries of Scotland

Open all year Mon–Sat 10-5 Sun 2-5. Admission free.
R, 100%, WC

East end of city centre, sales area, temporary exhibitions, wc, parties welcome booking preferred.

Housed in a striking gothic revival building by Rowand Anderson, the portraits of tragic Mary Queen of Scots, romantic Jacobites, philosopher David Hume, poet Robert Burns and writer Sir Walter Scott are amongst the many great Scots collected together in this gallery. Many are great works of art in their own right by artists like Ramsay, Reynolds, Gainsborough and Rodin. Recent commissions by the gallery include Her Majesty Queen Elizabeth The Queen Mother and Muriel Spark. An outstanding collection of Scottish photograpy includes 5,000 works by the pioneers Hill and Adamson. See National Gallery of Scotland for details of educational activities. Concerts and evening events are held occasionally.

SCOTTISH RECORD OFFICE

H.M. General Register House, Princes Street, Edinburgh EH1 3YY
Tel:(031) 556 6585

Open all year. Exhibitions Mon–Fri 10-4. Search rooms 9-4.45. Admission free.
PPA, R, 50%

City centre, sales area, temporary exhibitions, parties welcome but must book.

The entrance hall of this fine Georgian building has a changing programme of exhibitions throughout the year. During the summer there are also exhibitions in the Robert Adam Dome Gallery, noted for its magnificent ceiling.

SCOTTISH RECORD OFFICE

West Register House, Charlotte Square, Edinburgh
Tel:(031) 556 6585
Correspondence to Exhibitions Officer, H.M. General Register House, Princes Street, Edinburgh EH1 3YY.

Open all year. Exhibitions Mon–Fri 10-4. Search room 9-4.45. Admission free.
PPA, L, 100%

West end of city centre, sales area.

The history of the building, originally St. George's Church, goes back to the building of the New Town of Edinburgh. Now the Scottish Record Office branch repository, the building contains public exhibition and search facilities. A permanent exhibition of manuscripts illustrating Scottish history from the 12th century to the present day is on display in the front hall. The material ranges from medieval charters to modern government papers and includes the Declaration of Arbroath (1320), a contemporary copy of the National Covenant (1638) and the Articles of Union (1706).

SCOTTISH RUGBY UNION LIBRARY AND MUSEUM

Murrayfield, Edinburgh
Tel:(031) 337 9551

Scottish Rugby Union

Open all year Mon, Wed, Sun 2-4.30. Other times by appointment. Admission free.
P, L, 100%, WC, G

West of city centre at Murrayfield Ground, parking for cars & coaches, sales area, wc, parties welcome but must book.

A collection of historic jerseys, caps, balls, trophies, photographs and documents associated with the history and development of the game and the Scottish Rugby Union.

SCOTTISH UNITED SERVICES MUSEUM

Crown Square, The Castle, Edinburgh
Tel:(031) 225 7534

Trustees of the National Museums of Scotland

Open Apr–Sep Mon–Sat 9.30-6 Sun 11-6 Oct–Mar Mon–Sat 9.30-5 Sun 12.30-4.20. Admission free but charge for Castle.
PPA, ST, 100%, WC, G

In grounds of Edinburgh Castle, parking limited in summer, wc, parties welcome but must book.

Contains a fascinating collection of costume, weapons, personal relics and general items of equipment. New galleries opened in 1987 deal with the history of the Scottish soldier up to the First World War.

STILLS GALLERY

105 High Street, Edinburgh
Tel:(031) 557 1140

Scottish Photography Group

Open all year during exhibitions Tue-Sat 11-5.30.
Admission free.
ST, G

City centre in Royal Mile, sales area, temporary exhibitions, wc, parties welcome but must book.

A gallery which hosts national and international exhibitions of photography and related media aimed at promoting a better public understanding of photography, while encouraging and supporting related activities.

TALBOT RICE GALLERY

Old College, University of Edinburgh, Edinburgh EH8 9LY
Tel:(031) 667 1011 ex.4308

University of Edinburgh

Open all year Mon-Fri 10-5 also Sat 10-5 during exhibitions. Admission free.
100%, G

Near Royal Museum of Scotland, Chambers Street, parking nearby, sales area, temporary exhibitions, wc, parties welcome but must book.

A modern art gallery and permanent collection housed within a magnificent Georgian quadrangle. Temporary exhibitions, mainly of contemporary fine art (with an emphasis on one-man shows), are held regularly. The permanent collection includes 17th century paintings and bronzes.

THE PEOPLE'S STORY

Canongate Tolbooth, 163 Canongate, Edinburgh
Tel:(031) 225 2424 ex.6638

Edinburgh District Council

Open all year Mon-Sat 10-5 Jun-Sep 10-6. Admission free.
R, 50%, WC, G

Opposite Huntly House in Royal Mile, sales area, wc, parties welcome but must book.

The People's Story deals with the life and work of Edinburgh's people from the 1780s to the 1980s. It features sounds, smells and reconstructions, including a pub, tearoom, lodging house booth and wash house.

369 GALLERY

233 Cowgate, Edinburgh EH1 1NQ
Tel:(031) 225 3013

Board of Trustees

Open all year Mon-Sat 10.30-5.30. Admission free.
L, <50%

Near Royal Mile, sales area, temporary exhibitions, wc, parties welcome no need to book.

369 Gallery was founded in 1978 to promote contemporary painting in Scotland. Regular exhibitions by young Scottish artists are held in three separate galleries with occasional exchange exhibitions. Seven studios (one reserved for visiting artists) are in operation. There is an education room where daytime and evening classes are taught by resident artists.

HADDINGTON

JANE WELSH CARLYLE MUSEUM

Lodge Street, Haddington, East Lothian EH41 3EE
Tel:(062 082) 3738

Lamp of Lothian Trust

Open Apr-Sep Wed-Sat 2-5. Groups at other times by appointment. Admission charges.
ST, G

In town on A1 16 miles east of Edinburgh, wc, parties welcome but must book.

This late 18th century house is where Jane Welsh lived and met her husband, Thomas Carlyle, the famous writer and historian of the 19th century. Visitors have access to the elegant period drawing-room, exhibition room, conservatory and regency gardens.

LENNOXLOVE

Haddington, East Lothian EH41 4NZ
Tel:(062 082) 3720

Duke of Hamilton

Open Easter weekend, May-Sep Wed,Sat,Sun 2-5. Groups at other times by appointment. Admission charges (with concessions).
PPA, L/ST, <50%, G, C

18 miles east of Edinburgh, parking for cars & coaches, refreshments, sales area, wc, parties welcome but must book.

Home of the Duke and Duchess of Hamilton, this historic house contains many treasures including the Hamilton Palace Collection of furniture, paintings and porcelain, a portrait of La Belle Stewart (the model for Britannia on British coins) and Mary Queen of Scots' death mask, ring and silver casket. A herd of wild white cattle known as Cadzow Cattle, unique in Scotland, can be seen from the house. Booking forms for groups are available from the estate office.

LINLITHGOW

HOUSE OF THE BINNS

Linlithgow, West Lothian
Tel:(050 683) 4255

National Trust for Scotland

Open Easter weekend (excluding Fri) & May-Sep
Sat-Thu 2-5. Last admission 4.30. Admission charges
(with concessions). Parkland open all year.
PPA, L, 50%, G

15 miles west of Edinburgh off A904, parking for
cars & coaches, parties welcome but must book.

Set in grounds of 215 acres, the historic home
of the Dalyells dates from 1478 with major
17th century additions and reflects the early
17th century transition in Scottish architecture
from fortified stronghold to more spacious
mansion. Fine moulded plaster ceilings were
added in 1630. General Tam Dalyell raised the
Royal Scots Greys here in 1681.

LINLITHGOW PALACE

Linlithgow, West Lothian
Tel:(031) 244 3101 for information.

Scottish Development Department (Historic
Buildings and Monuments)

Open 3 Jan-Mar & Oct-Dec Mon-Sat 9.30-4 Sun 2-
4 Apr-Sep Mon-Sat 9.30-7 Sun 2-7. Admission
charges (with concessions).
P, L/ST, G

Town centre.

The palace where Mary Queen of Scots was
born and where all the Stewart Kings once
lived is now a ruin. A small display shows
some of the more interesting fragments of
architecture.

LINLITHGOW UNION CANAL SOCIETY

Canal Basin, Manse Road, Linlithgow, West Lothian
Correspondence to Mrs Aileen Lamb, 7 Friars Way,
Linlithgow, West Lothian. Tel:(0506) 842575.

Canal Society Limited

Open Easter-Sep Sat & Sun 2-5. Groups at other
times by appointment. Admission free to museum,
charges for boat trips.
PPA, R, 100%, WC, G

Beside Union Canal at Manse Road Bridge, parking
for cars, wc, parties welcome but must book.

This specialist museum, housed in old canal
stables, contains artefacts, photographs and an
audio-visual programme on the Edinburgh-
Glasgow Union Canal. Canal boat 'Victoria'
takes regular weekend trips and is available for
evening charter (12-20 people). Contact the
Canal Society for information on the cross-
Scotland canal marathons.

LIVINGSTON

ALMOND VALLEY HERITAGE CENTRE

Millfield, Kirkton, Livingston, West Lothian EH54
1AR
Tel:(0506) 414957

Almond Valley Heritage Trust

Open Easter-Oct daily 10-5. Admission charges.
P, L/R, 50%, WC, G, C, B

West of Livingston village off A705 at Mill
interchange, parking for cars & coaches, refreshments,
sales area, temporary exhibitions, wc, parties welcome
but must book.

This restored 18th century farm steading has
a childrens' farm and countryside museum, a
watermill, kiln, farm animals, farm and milling
machinery, bygones, and a riverside nature
trail. The Shale Oil Museum, opening in 1991,
will tell the story of the Scottish shale oil
industry.

NEWTONGRANGE

SCOTTISH MINING MUSEUM - LADY VICTORIA

Lady Victoria Colliery, Newtongrange, Midlothian
EH22 4QN
Tel:(031) 663 7519

Scottish Mining Museum Trust

Open all year Tue-Fri 10-4.30 Sat & Sun 12-5.
Admission charges (with concessions).
P, L, <50%, WC, G

On A7, parking for cars & coaches, refreshments,
sales area, wc, parties welcome but must book.

A recently renovated Victorian colliery. The
Grant Ritchie steam winding engine, the
largest in Scotland, can be operated by visitors.
Colliery and street scenes in the visitor centre
convey the sights, sounds and smells of colliery
life around the turn of the century. Library
and research facilities on all aspects of Scottish
mining history are available by arrangement.
See also Prestongrange under Prestonpans.

NORTH BERWICK

MUSEUM OF FLIGHT

East Fortune Airfield, nr. North Berwick, East Lothian
Tel:(062 088) 308
Correspondence to Royal Museum of Scotland, Chambers Street, Edinburgh EH1 1JF. Tel:(031) 225 7534.

Trustees of the National Museums of Scotland

Open 14 Apr-Sep daily 10.30-4.30. Admission free.
P, L, 100%, WC, G, C

22 miles east of Edinburgh off A1, parking for cars & coaches, sales area, temporary exhibitions, wc, parties welcome but must book.

A wide range of aircraft, aero-engines and rockets exhibited on a Second World War airfield. Collection includes the last Comet to fly in commercial colours, an Olympus jet engine (from Concorde) and a Blue Streak rocket. A special display features the R34 airship which took off from East Fortune in 1919 to make the first two-way flight across the Atlantic.

NORTH BERWICK MUSEUM

School Road, North Berwick, East Lothian
Tel:(0620) 3470
Correspondence to Library Headquarters, Lodge Street, Haddington EH41 3DX. Tel:(062 082) 4161.

East Lothian District Council

Open Easter-Sep Mon-Sat 10-1 & 2-5 Sun 2-5. Admission free.
P, ST, G

Signposted from town centre, parking for cars, sales area, temporary exhibitions, parties welcome no need to book.

A compact local museum with galleries devoted to golf, natural history, domestic history, archaeology and the history of the Royal Burgh of North Berwick.

PRESTONPANS

SCOTTISH MINING MUSEUM PRESTONGRANGE

Prestongrange, Prestonpans, East Lothian
Tel:(031) 665 9904

Scottish Mining Museum Trust

Open all year Tue-Fri 10-4 Sat & Sun 12-5. Admission free.
P, L, <50%, G, C

Between Musselburgh & Prestonpans on B1348, parking for cars & coaches, refreshments, wc, parties welcome but must book.

On a site with 800 years of mining history, the museum contains a Cornish beam engine (the last of its kind in Scotland) and changing exhibitions relating to the industrial heritage of the area. In 1990 the exhibition will be on industrial ceramics. See also Lady Victoria under Newtongrange.

SOUTH QUEENSFERRY

DALMENY HOUSE

South Queensferry, West Lothian
Tel:(031) 331 1888

Earl of Rosebery

Open May-Sep Sun-Thu 2-5.30. Admission charges.
P, ST, 100%, WC, G, C, B

7 miles west of Edinburgh & 3 miles east of South Queensferry on B924 (off A90), parking for cars & coaches, refreshments, sales area, temporary exhibitions, wc, parties welcome but must book.

A Tudor gothic revival house dating from 1814-17, beautifully situated on the shores of the Firth of Forth. Contains Rothschild collection of superb 18th century French furniture, tapestries and Sevres porcelain, Rosebery collection of fine 18th century portraits and other early paintings and furniture. Also the Napoleon room with a fascinating collection associated with the Emperor and the Duke of Wellington's campaign chair.

HOPETOUN HOUSE

South Queensferry EH30 9SL
Tel:(031) 331 2451

Hopetoun House Preservation Trust

Open 13 Apr-Sep daily 10-5.30. Admission charges.
P, ST, 50%, WC, G, C, B

3 miles west of South Queensferry on A904, parking for cars & coaches, refreshments, sales area, temporary exhibitions, wc, parties welcome but must book.

Set in magnificent parkland, Hopetoun has been the home of the Hope family since it was

20 Model of 'The Burry Man', an important part of local folklore at South Queensferry Museum. A local resident is selected as the Burry Man each year to parade through the town as part of an annual festival. *[Antonia Reeve]*

built in 1703. Enlargement of the house was carried out by William Adam and his sons John and Robert during the 18th century. The latter were also responsible for the interior decoration of the main apartments, much of which survives today. Sumptuous state rooms contain tapestries, furniture, rugs and paintings by Rubens, Titian, Canaletto and others. The only major decorative ceiling painting surviving from the baroque period in Scotland can be seen under the cupola. The house museum tells the story of the Hope family. 18th century stables contain exhibitions on the building of the house, and on wildlife and horses. The estate has a deer park, nature trails and a Ranger service.

QUEENSFERRY MUSEUM

Council Chambers, South Queensferry
Tel:(031) 331 1590
Correspondence to City Curator, Huntly House, 142 Canongate, Edinburgh EH8 8DD. Tel:(031) 225 2424 ex.6689.

Edinburgh District Council

Open all year Mon, Thu–Sat 10-1 & 2.15-5 Sun 12-5. Admission free.
ST, <50%, G

Village centre, parking for cars, parties welcome but must book.

The museum deals with the story of the historic Royal Burgh and of the river crossing, notably the two great bridges. There is a reconstruction of the famous 'Burry Man'.

Orkney Islands

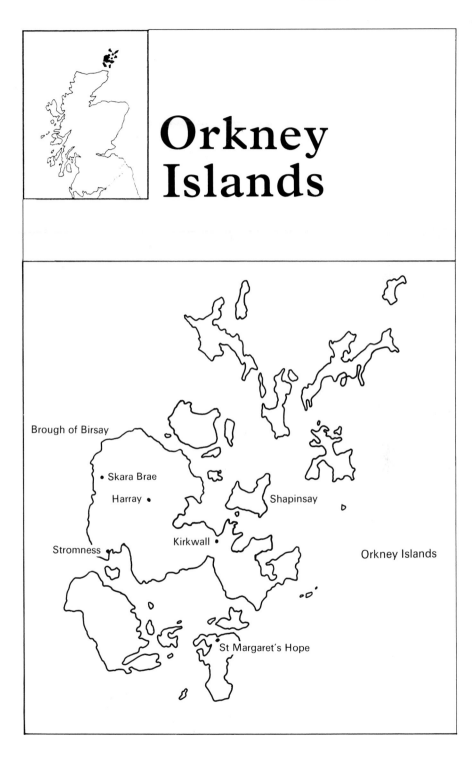

Brough of Birsay

• Skara Brae

Harray •

Shapinsay

Stromness •

Kirkwall •

Orkney Islands

St Margaret's Hope

BIRSAY

BROUGH OF BIRSAY

Orkney
Tel:(031) 244 3101 for information.

Scottish Development Department (Historic Buildings and Monuments)

Open Jan-Mar & Oct-Dec Wed-Sat 9.30-4 Sun-Tue 2-4 Apr-Sep Mon-Sat 9.30-7 Sun 2-7. Admission charges (with concessions).
G

On a tidal island 20 miles north west of Kirkwall.

A ruined Romanesque church alongside some interesting remains of Viking dwellings. A small site display contains some archaeological finds from the island.

ORKNEY FARM AND FOLK MUSEUM - KIRBUSTER

Kirbuster, Birsay, Orkney
Tel:(085 672) 268
Correspondence to Tankerness House Museum, Kirkwall, Orkney KW15 1DH.

Orkney Islands Council

Open Mar-Oct Mon-Sat 10.30-1 & 2-5 Sun 2-7. Admission charges (with concessions).
P, L/ST, 100%, G

Parking for cars & coaches, sales area, wc, parties welcome but must book.

This ancient farmstead includes the last surviving example of an Orkney 'firehoose' with its central hearth and stone 'neuk' bed. The complex includes a collection of farm implements and machinery, and a cottage garden.

HARRAY

ORKNEY FARM AND FOLK MUSEUM - CORRIGALL

Harray, Orkney
Tel:(085 677) 411
Correspondence to Tankerness House Museum, Kirkwall, Orkney KW15 1DH.

Orkney Islands Council

Open Mar-Oct Mon-Sat 10.30-1 & 2-5 Sun 2-7. Admission charges (with concessions).
P, L, 100%, G

2 miles east of Dounby & 1 mile off A986, parking for cars & coaches, sales area, wc, parties welcome but must book.

These restored 19th century Orkney farm buildings contain typical artefacts from that period including a grain drying kiln, hand mill and weaving loom. The 'click' mill nearby, in the care of the Scottish Development Department, is the only working example of an Orcadian horizontal water mill.

KIRKWALL

TANKERNESS HOUSE MUSEUM

Broad Street, Kirkwall, Orkney KW15 1DH
Tel:(0856) 3191

Orkney Islands Council

Open all year Mon-Sat 10.30-12.30 & 1.30-5 May-Sep also Sun 2-5. Admission charges (with concessions) Apr-Sep, free Oct-Mar.
L, <50%, G

Town centre, parking nearby, sales area, temporary exhibitions, wc, parties welcome but must book.

Standing opposite the 12th century St. Magnus Cathedral, Orkney's principal museum is housed in a 16th century merchant laird's house. Displays tell the history of the islands over the past 5,000 years with exhibits of international importance from the Stone, Bronze and Iron ages. Contains the Pictish Burrian symbol stone, St. Magnus reliquary from the Norse period and a variety of craft and trade items from the Middle Ages to the present day. Recently renewed Neolithic/Bronze Age galleries provide an excellent introduction to Orkney's outstanding ancient monuments. The fine walled garden is open at all times.

RONALDSAY

TOMB OF THE EAGLES

St.Margaret's Hope, Ronaldsay, Orkney
Tel:(085 683) 339

Private

Open Apr-Sep daily 10-8 Oct-Mar during daylight. Admission charges.
P, L/ST, G

South end of Ronaldsay, parking for cars & coaches, wc, parties welcome but must book.

Discovered by the Simison family, this 5,000 year-old tomb stands 3/4 mile away from their house. A showcase in their porch displays bones, tools, flint, pottery and beads found in the Stone Age Tomb. The tomb is associated with eagles because of the claws of the white-tailed eagle found buried with the occupants.

21   Tankerness House Museum's archaeology gallery includes this display on the 'Tomb of the Eagles', an important 5,000 year old site on Orkney. *[Tankerness House Museum]*

SHAPINSAY

BALFOUR CASTLE

Shapinsay, Orkney
Tel:(085 671) 282

Private

Open May-Sep Sun & Wed. See local press for details
of boat times from Kirkwall to Shapinsay, which
determine opening times. Admission charges include
cost of boat, an Orkney tea at the local castle, and
tour of the house and gardens.

Ferry to island, sales area, wc, parties welcome but
must book.

The house, built in 1848, contains portraits of
the Balfour family and a small local history
museum.

SKARA BRAE

SKARA BRAE

Orkney
Tel:(031) 244 3101 for information.

Scottish Development Department (Historic
Buildings and Monuments)

Open Jan-Mar & Oct-Dec Mon-Sat 9.30-4 Sun 2-4
Apr-Sep Mon-Sat 9.30-7 Sun 2-7. Admission charges
(with concessions).
G

9 miles north west of Kirkwall.

An impressive cluster of dwellings dating from
1400-1600 BC, preserved in drift sand until
uncovered by a storm in 1850. A small display
shows some of the finds associated with the
site.

ST MARGARET'S HOPE

OLD SMIDDY

Cromarty Square, St. Margaret's Hope, Orkney
Contact Stephen Manson, tel:(085 683) 366 for
further details.

South Ronaldsay & Burray Community Council

Open May-Sep daily 2-5. Other times by
appointment. Admission free.
P, R, 100%, G

This restored smiddy contains agricultural
machinery made by resident smiths over the
years, and the forge and tools they used.

AN ORKNEY WIRELESS MUSEUM

Church Road, St Margaret's Hope, Orkney
Tel:(0856) 83 462

Private

Open Apr-Sep daily 10-8. Admission charges (with
concessions).
L, 100%

On edge of village, wc.

A cottage museum showing a collection of
historic wireless and electrical equipment,
featuring wartime radio at Scapa Flow.
Displays include maps, charts, wartime
photographs and documents.

STROMNESS

PIER ARTS CENTRE

Victoria Street, Stromness, Orkney KW16 3AA
Tel:(0856) 850209

Pier Arts Centre Trust

Open all year Tue-Sat 10.30-12.30 & 1.30-5
Jun,Jul,Aug also Sun & Mon 2-5. Admission free.
L, 50%, G

Town centre, sales area, temporary exhibitions, wc,
parties welcome but must book.

This modern art gallery is housed in two
18th century buildings, a house and warehouse
backing on to the pier. A collection of paintings
which includes works by Ben Nicholson,
Barbara Hepworth and Alfred Wallis is on
permanent display. There is a regular, lively
programme of temporary exhibitions. A special
feature of the gallery is the Childrens' Room
where younger visitors can produce and display
their own work.

STROMNESS MUSEUM

52 Alfred St, Stromness, Orkney
Tel:(0856) 850025

Orkney Natural History Society

Open all year Mon-Sat 10.30-12.30 & 1.30-5.
Admission charges.
L, <50%, G

South end of town, parking for cars, sales area.

The natural and maritime history of Orkney.
Collections include birds, butterflies, shells,
and fossils. There are displays on whaling,
fishing, Scapa Flow and the German Fleet.
There is also an extensive photographic
archive.

Inveraray Jail, the dramatically-situated 19th century prison which now houses a museum re-creating prison life. [*Inveraray Jail Museum*]

The Denny Ship Model Experimental Tank, an historic building where designs for many famous vessels were tested for seaworthiness. Now part of the Scottish Maritime Museum. [*Scottish Maritime Museum*]

'Princess Cecily', stained glass portrait on view at the Burrell Collection, Glasgow. [*Scottish Museums Council*]

One of the spacious galleries at the Burrell Collection, Glasgow. [*Scottish Museums Council*]

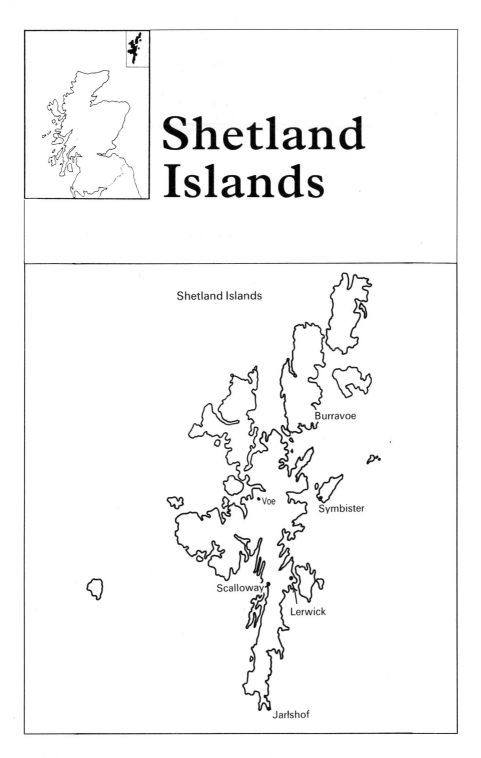

Shetland Islands

Shetland Islands

Burravoe

Voe

Symbister

Scalloway

Lerwick

Jarlshof

DUNROSSNESS

SHETLAND CROFT HOUSE MUSEUM

Voe, Dunrossness, Shetland
Correspondence to Shetland Museum, Lower Hillhead, Lerwick ZE1 0EL. Tel:(0595) 5057.

Shetland Islands Council

Open May-Sep Tue-Sun 10-1 & 2-5. Admission charges.
G

Four miles north of Sumburgh Airport off A970, parking for cars & coaches, sales area, wc, parties welcome but must book.

A croft, house, steading and mill restored and furnished in the style of the late 19th century.

FAIR ISLE

GEORGE WATERSON MEMORIAL CENTRE

Fair Isle, Shetland

George Waterson Memorial Centre Association

Open May-Sep by arrangement. Contact the Chairman, tel:(03512) 244. Admission free.
L, 100%, G

Flight or ferry to island, parking for cars, sales area, temporary exhibitions, parties welcome but must book.

This centre opened in Spring 1986. Due to limited flight and ferry timetables visitors are shown round on request only. Special features of the centre include displays associated with an isolated island crofting community and with fishing and locally crafted small boats.

GOTT

TINGWALL AGRICULTURAL MUSEUM

Veensgarth, Gott, Shetland ZE2 9SB
Tel:(059 584) 344

Jeanie Sandison

Open Jun-Sep Tue,Thu,Sat 10-1 & 2-5 Wed 10-1, Sun 2-5. Other times by arrangement. Admission charges (with concessions).
ST, G

5 miles from Lerwick off A971, parking for cars & coaches, sales area, temporary exhibitions, wc, parties welcome but must book.

A folk museum housed in the 19th century granary, bothy and stables of a working croft. The collection contains tools, equipment and various horse-drawn implements relating to the work of the Shetland crofter of the past.

LERWICK

BOD OF GREMISTA (BOOTH OF GREMISTA)

Lerwick, Shetland
Correspondence to T.M.Y. Manson, 93 Gilbertson Road, Lerwick, Shetland.

Bod of Gremista Restoration Committee

Opening details from Tourist Office. Admission charges.
PPA, L, 100%, G

On northern outskirts of Lerwick, parking for cars, parties welcome but must book.

A late 18th/early 19th century booth associated with the Shetland fishing industry, this building was also the birthplace of Arthur Anderson, co-founder and chief developer of the Peninsular & Oriental Steam Navigation Company and a benefactor to education in London, Southampton and his native islands. The museum illustrates his life and times.

SHETLAND MUSEUM

Lower Hillhead, Lerwick ZE1 0EL
Tel:(0595) 5057

Shetland Islands Council

Open all year Mon,Wed,Fri 10-7 Tue,Thu,Sat 10-5. Admission free.
P, L, WC, G

Town centre, parking for cars & coaches, sales area, temporary exhibitions, wc, parties welcome no need to book.

Shetland life through the ages is the theme of this museum, which has an outstanding collection of ship and boat models and material from several historic wreck sites. Folk life, archaeology and Shetland textiles are covered in the other main displays. Regular programme of lectures organised.

22   The Hanseatic Booth, Shetland. *[Scottish Museums Council]*

23   Interior of the Hanseatic Booth, Shetland. *[Scottish Museums Council]*

SCALLOWAY

SCALLOWAY MUSEUM

Main Street, Scalloway, Shetland

Scalloway History Group

Open May-Sep Sun,Tue,Wed,Thu 2-5 Sat 10-1 & 2-5. Other times by arrangement, tel:(0595 88) 256 or 675. Admission free.

P, L, >50%, G

7 miles west of Lerwick, parking for cars & coaches, sales area, temporary exhibitions, wc, parties welcome but must book.

A varied collection from Scalloway and the surrounding area covering prehistory to modern times. The museum includes displays on the Shetland Bus (the Norwegian resistance in the Second World War) and local industries, in particular fishing. It contains a wide selection of photographs.

SUMBURGH HEAD

JARLSHOF

Shetland
Tel:(031) 244 3101 for information.

Scottish Development Department (Historic Buildings and Monuments)

Open 3 Jan-Mar & Oct-Dec Mon & Thu-Sat 9.30-4 Sun & Tue-Wed 2-4 Apr-Sep Mon & Thu-Sat 9.30-7 Sun & Tue-Wed 2-7. Admission charges (with concessions).

P, ST, 50%, G

At Sumburgh Head approx 22 miles south of Lerwick.

One of the most remarkable archaeological sites in Britain contains the remains of three extensive village settlements occupied from the Bronze Age to Viking times.

SYMBISTER

THE PIER HOUSE (HANSEATIC BOOTH)

Symbister, Whalsay, Shetland ZE1 9AA
Secretary J.A. Anderson Tel:(0595) 3535 ex.315

Hanseatic Booth Trust

Mon-Sat 9-1 & 2-5, Sun 2-4. Collect key from Bremen Cafe or 'Harbour View'. Admission charges (with concessions).

L/ST, 50%, G

On island of Whalsay, parking for cars & coaches.

The Pier House commemorates the trade links between Shetland and the Hanseatic Ports of Hamburg, Bremen and Lubeck from the Middle Ages to the early 18th century. Displays tell the story of this trade and a reconstruction shows the types of goods traded. There is also a general section on Whalsay.

YELL

OLD HAA

Burravoe, Yell, Shetland ZE2 9AY
Tel:(095 782) 339
Correspondence to Mrs. Garriock, Brunthill, Burravoe, Yell, Shetland. Tel:(095 782) 225.

Old Haa Trustees

Open all year Tue-Thu, Sat 10-4 Sun 2-5. Admission free.

P, L, <50%, G, C

Parking for cars & coaches, refreshments, sales area, temporary exhibitions, wc, parties welcome but must book.

A small museum and gallery with changing exhibitions of arts and crafts and local history. There are video and audio tapes of Shetland music and folklore, and photographs of past Shetland life.

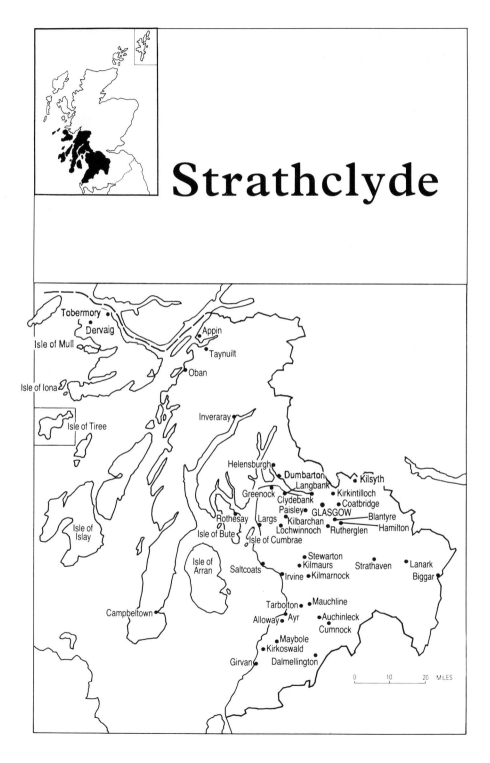

Strathclyde

ALLOWAY

BURNS' COTTAGE & MUSEUM

Alloway, Ayr, KA7 4PY
Tel:(0282) 41215

Trustees of Burns' Monument & Cottage

Open all year Spring & Autumn Mon-Sat 10-5 Sun 2-5 Summer Mon-Sat 9-7 Sun 10-7 Winter Mon-Sat 10-4. Admission charges (with concessions).
P, L, 100%, G, C

2 miles south of Ayr on B7024, parking for cars & coaches, refreshments, sales area, wc, parties welcome but must book.

The birthplace of Robert Burns (1759-1796), this museum contains many relics and manuscripts belonging to Scotland's national poet as well as a large reference library.

BURNS' MONUMENT & GARDENS

Alloway, Ayr, KA7 4PQ
Tel:(0292) 41321

Trustees of Burns' Monument & Cottage

Open all year Apr-Oct daily 9-5 Nov-Mar 10-5. Admission charges (with concessions).
ST, <50%, G

2 miles south of Ayr on B7024, parking for cars & coaches, sales area, wc, parties welcome.

Built in 1823, this monument and museum contains relics, books and manuscripts associated with Robert Burns.

LAND O'BURNS CENTRE

Murdoch's Lone, Alloway, Ayrshire
Tel:(0292) 43700

Kyle & Carrick District Council

Open all year daily Oct-May 10-5 Jun & Sep 1-5.30 Jul & Aug 10-6. Admission free but charge for a-v programme.
P, L/R, 100%, WC, E, G, C

South of Ayr on B7024, parking for cars & coaches, tea room, sales area, temporary exhibitions, wc, parties welcome but must book.

An interpretation centre at the beginning of the Burns Heritage Trail with exhibits and audio-visual programme on the life and works of the poet.

THE ROZELLE GALLERIES

Rozelle Park, Monument Road, Alloway, Ayr KA7 4NQ
Tel:(0292) 45447 or 43708

Kyle & Carrick District Library & Museum Services / Mrs Maclaurin's Trust

Open all year Mon-Sat 10-5 Apr-Oct also Sun 2-5. Admission free.
P, L/ST, <50%, G, C

South of Ayr off B7024 400 metres from Burns' Cottage, parking for cars & coaches, refreshments, sales area, temporary exhibitions, wc, parties welcome no need to book.

Set in spacious parkland these two galleries occupy the house and stables of Rozelle House. The Maclaurin Gallery, housed in the converted stable block, has continuous temporary exhibitions of fine and applied art. An expanding collection of contemporary art is on permanent display in the main house together with local history and military exhibits. The grounds contain sculpture including work by Henry Moore, woodland walks and sports facilities.

APPIN

CASTLE STALKER

Appin, Argyll
Tel:(063 173) 234
Correspondence to Lt. Col. D.R. Stewart Allward, 65 Westhall Road, Warlingham, Surrey CR3 9YE. Tel:(0883) 623944.

Lt. Col. D.R. Stewart Allward

Open during summer months by appointment. Admission charges.

Between Oban & Ballachulish on A828, parking for cars & coaches, parties welcome but must book.

This fine example of a 16th century Scottish keep·has associations with James IV and V and contains an impressive display of historic weapons.

AUCHINLECK

AUCHINLECK BOSWELL MUSEUM & MAUSOLEUM

Church Hill (Kirk Brae), Auchinleck, Ayrshire
Correspondence to The Secretary, Mr. Colin McDonald, R.D. Hunter & Co., 1 The Square, Cumnock KA18 1BQ. Tel:(0290) 21185.

Auchinleck Boswell Society

Open Easter-end Sep by appointment. Admission free.
P, L, 50%

Auchinleck on A76, parking for cars & coaches, parties welcome but must book.

A memorial museum to two famous Auchinleck sons: James Boswell (1740-1795) the biographer of Dr. Johnson; and William Murdoch (1754-1839) who developed the use of gas for lighting.

BIGGAR

BIGGAR GASWORKS

Gasworks Road, Biggar, Lanarkshire
Tel:(0899) 21070
Correspondence to Royal Museum of Scotland, Chambers Street, Edinburgh EH1 1JF. Tel:(031) 225 7534.

Trustees of the National Museums of Scotland

Open Jun-Sep Mon-Thu 2-5 Sat-Sun 12-5. Other times by appointment. Admission free.
P, ST, 100%, G

Off High Street, parking nearby, sales area, parties welcome but must book.

Biggar Gasworks was built in 1839 to supply the streets and houses of Biggar with gas lighting. It closed in 1973 when the town was converted to natural gas. Now an ancient monument in the guardianship of Historic Buildings and Monuments (Scottish Development Department) it is being developed as a museum in collaboration with the National Museums of Scotland. Besides the gasworks itself, gas lighting, steam engines, gas appliances and other machinery are on display.

GLADSTONE COURT MUSEUM

Biggar ML12 6DT
Tel:(0899) 21050

Biggar Museum Trust

Open Easter-Oct Mon-Sat 10-12.30 & 2-5 Sun 2-5. Admission charges (with concessions).
P, L, 100%, G

Town centre, parking nearby, refreshments, sales area, wc, parties welcome but must book.

Begun in an old coachworks, Gladstone Court has expanded over the years to become a fascinating recreation of a 19th/early 20th century street. Traders such as the grocer, dressmaker, chemist and bootmaker along with the bank, village library, photographer's booth and schoolroom illustrate the differences and similarities between life 100 years ago and life today. Special activities for schools and leaflets in French and German are available.

GREENHILL COVENANTERS' HOUSE

Burn Braes, Biggar ML12 6DT
Tel:(0899) 21050

Biggar Museum Trust

Open Apr-mid Oct daily 2-5. Other times by appointment. Admission charges (with concessions).
P, L, <50%, G, AD

Town centre, parking for cars & coaches, sales area, parties welcome but must book.

The story of the Covenanters (from 1603-1707) is told in this old house, the residence of Lady Greenhill at that time. Displays include a reconstruction of the library of Andrew Hay, the local diarist, a kitchen complete with press bed, a four-poster bed, coins, banners and Bibles. Rare breeds of sheep, pigs and poultry are kept in the grounds. Schools activities are arranged at this award-winning museum and a video film on the Scottish Covenant is presented. Regular Rare Breed Open Days and Civil War Musters are held.

MOAT PARK HERITAGE CENTRE

Biggar ML12 6DT
Tel:(0899) 21050

Biggar Museum Trust

Open Apr-Oct Mon-Sat 10-5 Sun 2-5 Nov-Mar Mon-Fri 9-5. Other times by arrangement. Admission charges (with concessions).
P, ST, 50%, WC, G

Biggar 30 miles from Edinburgh on A702, parking, temporary exhibitions, not yet suitable for parties.

Flagship of a growing number of museums in the area, Moat Park was opened by HRH The Princess Royal in 1988. Displays cover the geology of the upper Clyde and Tweed valleys, and present a microcosm of life in the Biggar area from 7,000 years ago to the present. There is also a display of patchwork and embroidery, including an enormous tailor's quilt. Museum leaflets are available in French and English. Appointments can be made here to use the Albion Archive, the complete records of Albion Motors, Scottish commercial vehicle manufacturers founded at Biggar in 1899. The archives contain records and photographs from that time to the 1970's.

BISHOPBRIGGS

THOMAS MUIR MUSEUM

Bishopbriggs Library, 170 Kirkintilloch Road, Bishopbriggs, Glasgow
Correspondence to Strathkelvin District Museums,

The Cross, Kirkintilloch, Glasgow G66 1AB. Tel:(041) 775 1185.

Strathkelvin District Council

Open all year Mon,Tue,Thu,Fri 9.45-8 Wed 9.45-1 & 2-5 Sat 9.45-1. Admission free.

P, ST, 100%

Parking for cars.

This small museum tells the story of Thomas Muir, the mid-18th century radical lawyer who was sentenced to 14 years transportation in Botany Bay for agitating for parliamentary reform. He escaped and journeyed around the world before dying at the age of 33 in revolutionary Paris.

BLANTYRE

DAVID LIVINGSTONE CENTRE

Blantyre, Glasgow G72 9BT
Tel:(0698) 823140

Scottish National Memorial to David Livingstone

Open all year Mon-Sat 10-6 Sun 2-6. Admission charges (with concessions).

P, ST, 50%, WC, G, C

Blantyre on A74, parking for cars & coaches, refreshments, sales area, temporary exhibitions, wc, parties welcome, booking preferred.

Situated at Blantyre on the banks of the River Clyde, the centre is enclosed in 8 acres of wooded parkland with gardens, picnic and play areas. The permanent exhibition of objects, maps, journals etc. depict the life of David Livingstone, the great Scottish explorer and missionary, and is housed in the original 18th century tenement building in which he was born. There is a social history museum adjoining. Changing exhibitions on modern Africa are mounted each year from April to September in the Africa Pavilion.

BRODICK

BRODICK CASTLE & GARDEN, GOATFELL & COUNTRY PARK

Brodick, Isle of Arran
Tel:(0770) 2202

National Trust for Scotland

Open mid Apr-Sep daily 1-5 Oct Mon,Wed,Sat 1-5. Garden & Country park all year 9.30-sunset. Admission charges (with concessions).

P, L, 50%, WC, G, C

2 miles from Brodick Pier & 15 miles from Lochranza, ferry from Ardrossan to Brodick (1 hour), ferry from Kintyre summer only, parking for cars & coaches, refreshments sales area, wc, parties welcome but must book.

The ancient seat of the Dukes of Hamilton and recently the home of the late Duchess of Montrose contains superb silver, porcelain 'objets d'art' associated with William Beckford and a collection of paintings including many 19th century sporting works. Gardens and nature trail are an added attraction.

ISLE OF ARRAN HERITAGE MUSEUM

Rosaburn, Brodick, Isle of Arran KA27 8DP
Tel:(0770) 2636

Correspondence to Secretary, Mrs. Alexander, Sinnavoe, Brodick, Isle of Arran.

Isle of Arran Museum Trust

Open late Apr-end Sep Mon-Sat 10.30-1 & 2-4.30 also Oct by arrangement. Admission charges (with concessions).

P, L, 100%, G, C

1 mile from Brodick Pier, parking for cars & coaches, refreshments, sales area, temporary exhibitions, wc, parties welcome but must book.

This museum is housed in traditional farm buildings set beside a river. The cottage is furnished in late 19th and early 20th century styles. A blacksmith's shop, a milk house complete with dairying equipment and a stable block with displays of local history, archaeology, geology and farm implements are amongst the exhibits. Arran High School Heritage Projects are also exhibited here. Spinning, lace-making and weaving demonstrations are held occasionally.

CAMPBELTOWN

CAMPBELTOWN MUSEUM

Hall Street, Campbeltown, Argyll
Tel:(0586) 52366 ex.218

Argyll & Bute District Council

Open all year Mon,Tue,Thu,Fri 10-1 & 2-5 & 6-8 Wed,Sat 10-1 & 2-5. Admission free.

Town centre, wc, not suitable for parties.

Housed within the town library in an attractive 19th century building, this small museum displays local archaeological finds, natural history and has a collection of fishing boat models.

24   Tram used to transport visitors around the open-air site at Summerlee Heritage Park, Coatbridge. *[Summerlee Heritage Trust]*

CLYDEBANK

CLYDEBANK DISTRICT MUSEUM

Old Town Hall, Dumbarton Road, Clydebank G81 1XQ
Tel:(041) 941 1331 ex 402
Correspondence to Librarian, Clydebank District Libraries, Dumbarton Road, Clydebank G81 1XH. Tel:(041) 952 1416.

Clydebank District Council

Open all year Mon,Wed 2-4.30 Sat 10-4.30. Groups at other times by appointment. Admission free.
ST, 100%, G

Town centre, parking for cars & coaches, sales area, temporary exhibitions, wc, parties welcome but must book.

A small museum situated beside the shipyards where some of the world's greatest liners were built. The permanent displays tell the story of the shipbuilders and the town which grew up around the yards. The museum also has a large specialist collection of sewing machines.

COATBRIDGE

SUMMERLEE HERITAGE PARK

West Canal Street, Coatbridge ML5 1QD
Tel:(0236) 31261

Summerlee Heritage Trust

Open daily 10-5. Admission free.
P, L/R, 100%, WC, G, C

Town centre between Sunnyside & Coatbridge stations, parking for cars & coaches, refreshments, sales, temporary exhibitions, wc, parties welcome.

Summerlee interprets the social and industrial history of Central Scotland, and in particular the Monklands area, formerly the 'Iron Burgh'. Displays feature historic machinery in daily operation as well as reconstructed domestic environments. Scotland's only working electric tramway provides transport round a 25 acre site giving access to a restored section of the Monkland Canal, an operating boatshop, tram depot, steam cranes and railway locomotives and archaeological excavation of 1830's ironworks, whilst a coal mine is under construction. There is an annual programme of special events including a Steam Fair, Historic Vehicle Rally and Canal Festival.

CUMNOCK

BAIRD INSTITUTE MUSEUM

Lugar Street, Cumnock KA18 1AD
Tel:(0290) 22111

Cumnock & Doon Valley District Council

Open all year Fri 9.30-1 & 1.30-4 Sat 11-1. Other
times by appointment. Admission free.
ST, G

Town centre on A76, sales area, temporary
exhibitions, wc, parties welcome but must book.

A local history museum containing wooden
ware and local pottery with a lively temporary
exhibition programme. Schools, clubs,
organisations are made welcome at any time
by prior arrangement. Worksheets and audio-
visual presentations are available for children.

DALMELLINGTON

CATHCARTSON VISITOR CENTRE

8-11 Cathcartston, Dalmellington, Ayr KA6 7QY
Tel:(0292) 550633
Correspondence to Secretary, A.E. Joss, 2 Ayr Road,
Dalmellington, Ayr KA6 7SJ.

Dalmellington & District Conservation Trust

Open all year Mon-Fri 10-4 Sat,Sun 2-5. Other times
by appointment. Admission free.
P, R, 100%, G

15 miles from Ayr on the A713, parking for cars &
coaches, sales area, temporary exhibitions, wc, parties
welcome book from Oct-Mar.

Opened in 1985 this row of weavers' cottages,
dated 1744, has been converted to provide an
exhibition area and a small museum of the
weaving period featuring an 18th century loom,
a kitchen display and a slide show. Town,
countryside and industrial trails can be
arranged by contacting the Secretary. Facilities
can be provided for school pupils and students.

CHAPEL ROW IRON-WORKERS COTTAGES

Waterside, Dalmellington, Ayr KA6
Correspondence to Secretary, A.E. Joss, 2 Ayr Road,
Dalmellington, Ayr KA6 7SJ.

Dalmellington & District Conservation Trust

Open all year Mon-Fri 10-4 Sat,Sun 2-5. Other times
by appointment. Admission charges.
R/ST, 100%, G

15 miles from Ayr on A713.

Two cottages built for iron workers are being
converted, one furnished as a workers' cottage,
and the other as an exhibition area.

DERVAIG

THE OLD BYRE HERITAGE/VISITOR CENTRE

Dervaig, Isle of Mull, Argyll PA75 6QR
Tel:(068 84) 229

Mr & Mrs J M Bradley

Open daily Easter-mid Oct 10.30-6. Admission
charges.
P, ST, <50%, G

Outskirts of village, parking for cars & coaches,
refreshments, sales area, wc.

This centre has displays on the natural history
of Mull, supported by a series of audio-visual
programmes, covering the geology, history and
wildlife of the island.

DUMBARTON

DENNY SHIP MODEL EXPERIMENT TANK BUILDING

Castle Street, Dumbarton
Correspondence to Scottish Maritime Museum,
Laird Forge, Gottries Road, Irvine KA12 8QE.
Tel:(0294) 78283.

Scottish Maritime Museum

Open all year Mon-Fri 9-5. Weekends by
appointment. Admission charges (with concessions).

Off Glasgow Road, parking for cars, temporary
exhibitions, parties welcome but must book.

Built to the design of William Froude in 1883
the Denny Tank was the first ship model tank
testing establishment to be constructed in a
commercial shipyard. Such varied craft as
Sir Thomas Lipton's 'Shamrock', the 'Queen
Mary' and the battleship 'Vanguard' were
amongst the thousands tested during its 100
year existence. The equipment includes the
original model-shaping machine, the carriage
containing recording equipment and a wave-
making machine. The tank itself is part of a
building complex which includes workshop
areas and a drawing office. A guided tour is
provided for all visitors.

EASDALE ISLAND

EASDALE ISLAND FOLK MUSEUM

Easdale Island, off Seil Island, by Oban, Argyll
Correspondence to Jean Adams, 5 Easdale Island, by
Oban, Argyll. Tel:(085 23) 370 (evenings).

C.P.R. Nicholson

Open Apr-Oct weekdays 10.30-5.30 Sun 10.30-4.30.
Admission charges.
ST, 100%, G

Regular passenger service to island, parking on
mainland, wc, parties welcome no need to book.

A pictorial history of the slate island in the
19th century shows the industrial and domestic
life of the villagers. Other exhibits include
'Kirsty's' kitchen, domestic items and
equipment used in the slate industry. The
museum contains microfilms of records dating
back to 1745 and papers relating to the Friendly
Societies and the 1st Argyll & Bute Artillery
Volunteers. Scenic walk to the sea-filled slate
quarries nearby which were devastated by the
great storm of November 1881.

GIRVAN

McKECHNIE INSTITUTE

Dalrymple Street, Girvan, Ayrshire KA26 9AE
Tel:(0465) 3643

Girvan Community Council & Kyle and Carrick
District Council

Open all year Tue-Sat 10-4 Jul-Aug also Mon 11-4.
Admission free.
L/ST, 50%, G

Centre of Girvan 20 miles south of Ayr on A77,
parking nearby, sales area, temporary exhibitions,
wc, parties welcome but must book.

This red sandstone building with octagonal
tower first opened in 1888 as a subscription
library and now functions as a local museum
and community arts centre. Recent acquisitions
include the ship's wheel and other relics from
the 'SS Wallachia', a 19th century cargo ship
sunk off Argyll and discovered by the Girvan
Sub-Aqua Club in 1977. Temporary
exhibitions relate to the crafts, local history
and natural history of Carrick district.
Exhibitions by local artists held regularly. The
permanent collection of paintings is composed
mainly of late Victorian bequests to the former
Burgh of Girvan.

GLASGOW

ART GALLERY & MUSEUM, KELVINGROVE

Glasgow G3 8AG
Tel:(041) 357 3929

City of Glasgow District Council

Open all year Mon-Fri 10-5 Sat 10-10 Sun 12-6.
Admission free.
P, L/ST, 100%, WC, G

West of city centre, parking for cars & coaches,
refreshments, sales area, temporary exhibitions, wc,
parties welcome no need to book.

Selections from one of the finest civic art
collections in Britain are displayed with items
from the decorative art and history collections
in galleries arranged thematically with the
titles: The Classical Tradition; The Art of the
Church; The Realist Tradition and Art and
Design: the Victorian Age and The Modern
Period. The museum contains internationally
significant collections of European arms and
armour, ethnography and Scottish and
Egyptian archaeology. The natural science
collections come from throughout the world.
Displays include a geology gallery,
introduction to the history of plant life on
earth, bird room, and an area devoted to
Scottish wildlife. Competitions and activities
for children and a programme of lectures
and talks. Contact the Museum Education
Department (tel:(041) 334 1131) for details
of lessons for school parties, annual young
people's art competition and other activities.

BURRELL COLLECTION

Pollok Country Park, 2060 Pollokshaws Road,
Glasgow G43 1AT
Tel:(041) 649 7151

City of Glasgow District Council

Open all year Mon,Tue,Thu-Sat 10-5 Wed 10-10
Sun 12-6. Admission free.
P, R, 100%, WC, WS, G, C, B, AD

South side of city in park, parking for cars & coaches,
refreshments, sales area, temporary exhibitions, wc,
parties welcome no need to book.

Visited by millions since it opened in 1983, the
collection housed in this unique custom-built
museum set in beautiful parkland was gifted
to the city of Glasgow in 1944 by Sir William
Burrell, a wealthy shipowner. Designed by
Barry Gasson, the building is constructed in
stone, timber and glass and incorporates
medieval architectural stonework. More than
8000 items covering the ancient world, oriental
art, European decorative arts and pictures from
the medieval period to the 20th century have
been brought together under one roof. The
Chinese ceramics and bronzes, the medieval
tapestries and stained glass and the 19th
century French paintings are of outstanding
quality. Daily free guided tours, temporary
exhibition programme, reference facilities,
lunchtime and evening events, picnic area are
amongst the many extra facilities. Contact the
Museum Education Department (tel:(041) 649
9929) for details of educational activities.

CHARLES RENNIE MACKINTOSH SOCIETY

Queen's Cross, 870 Garscube Road, Glasgow G20 7EL
Tel:(041) 946 6600 or (0360) 50595

Charles Rennie Mackintosh Society

Open all year Tue,Thu,Fri 12-5.30 Sun 2.30-5. Admission free.
P, ST, G

City centre, parking for cars & coaches, refreshments, sales area, temporary exhibitions, wc, parties welcome but must book.

The headquarters of the Charles Rennie Mackintosh Society are housed in this fine Mackintosh church (1897-99) on lease from the Church of Scotland. An extensive restoration programme is currently in process. Information centre and a reference library are open to visitors. Group tours can be arranged by contacting the director.

COLLINS GALLERY

University of Strathclyde, Glasgow G1 1XQ
Tel:(041) 552 4400 ex.2416

University of Strathclyde

Open all year Mon-Fri 10-5 Sat 12-4. Admission free.
PPA, L/ST, 100%, WC, G, C, AD

City centre close to George Square, parking for cars, sales area, temporary exhibitions, wc, parties welcome no need to book.

A temporary exhibition gallery specialising in 20th century arts.

GLASGOW PRINT STUDIO

22 King Street, Glasgow G1 5QP
Tel:(041) 552 0704

Glasgow Print Studio Council of Management

Open all year Mon-Sat 10-5.30. Admission free.
L/ST, 100%, WC, G

City centre east of George Square, parking nearby, sales area, temporary exhibitions, wc, parties welcome but must book.

This gallery has monthly exhibitions ranging from print shows to the work of Paolozzi, Ernst and Bellany. Visitors are welcome to visit the adjoining print workshops. Original prints created in these workshops are always on display. Introductory courses in etching, lithography, screenprinting and photography are held three times a year and are open to the public.

GLASGOW SCHOOL OF ART

167 Renfrew Street, Glasgow G3 6RQ
Tel:(041) 332 9797

Governors of the Glasgow School of Art

Open Term-time Mon-Thur 9.30-8, Fri 9.30-5, Sat 10-12. Non term-time Mon-Fri 9.30-4.30, Sat 10-12. Admission free.
R/ST, 100%, WC, G, C

Signposted from Sauchiehall Street, sales area, temporary exhibitions, wc, parties welcome but must book.

One of Charles Rennie Mackintosh's most outstanding buildings, the Glasgow School of Art houses not only original furniture and fittings designed by Mackintosh but also a substantial collection of his watercolours and architectural drawings. Furniture from Windyhill and Miss Cranston's Tea Rooms are also on display. The board room, director's room, library and Mackintosh furniture gallery are all open to visitors. There is also a temporary exhibition programme in the Mackintosh museum and Newber Gallery. National Trust guided tours of the building are available at certain times, for which a charge is made.

GLASGOW'S GLASGOW

Midland Street, The Arches, Glasgow
Tel:(041) 204 3993
Correspondence to: The Words and the Stones, 50 Washington Street, Glasgow

The Words & the Stones

Open 1990 only 13 Apr-5 Nov Tue-Sun 10-8. Admission charges (with concessions).
L, 100%, WC, C, B, AD

Behind Central Station in city centre, parking for cars & coaches, refreshments, sales area, wc.

Glasgow's Glasgow is a special exhibition for Glasgow's year as European City of Culture 1990. Over 2,000 artefacts connected with the history of Glasgow gathered from over 220 lenders throughout the world are installed in the Arches beneath the British Rail Central Station. Sound-cones, audio-visual monitors, interactive exhibits and live actors will enhance the exhibition which reflects Glasgow's history of trade and cultural connections around the world.

HAGGS CASTLE

100 St. Andrew's Drive, Glasgow G41 4RB
Tel:(041) 427 2725

City of Glasgow District Council

Open all year Mon-Sat 10-5 Sun 2-5. Admission free.
L, <50%, WC, G

25   Examining part of the extensive and important fossil collections of the Hunterian Museum, University of Glasgow. *[Hunterian Museum]*

South side of the city in Pollokshields, sales area, temporary exhibitions, wc, parties welcome but must book.

A history museum designed with children in mind, but fun for adults too. Features include a Victorian nursery, a 16th century kitchen, a 17th century bedroom and an exhibition about Mary Queen of Scots. Crafts workshops for children are held regularly and there is a picnic area.

HEATHERBANK MUSEUM OF SOCIAL WORK

163 Mugdock Road, Glasgow G62
Tel:(041) 956 2687

Trustees of the Heatherbank Museum

Open all year Mon,Wed,Fri 10-12 Tue,Thu,Sun 2-5. Other times by appointment. Admission free.
P, L, 100%, G, AD

Milngavie on A81 north of Glasgow centre, parking for cars, parties welcome but must book.

Small specialist museum with a fascinating display of objects, models, photographs and ephemera relating to the history of social work in Scotland. A reference and picture library deals with all aspects of the history of social work in Scotland.

HUNTERIAN ART GALLERY

University of Glasgow, Glasgow G12 8QQ
Tel:(041) 330 5431

University of Glasgow

Open all year Mon-Fri 9.30-5 Sat 9.30-1 May-Oct also Sat 9.30-5 Sun 2-5. Admission free except for a charge for Mackintosh House on weekday afternoons and Sat.
PPA, R/ST, >50%, G, C

West end of city, parking nearby, coaches must book, refreshments sales area, temporary exhibitions, wc, parties welcome but must book.

A gallery with outstanding collections of work by J M Whistler and C R Mackintosh including 'The Mackintosh House', a reconstruction on 3 levels of the architect's home fitted with his own furniture. The main gallery displays Old Masters including Rembrandt, Chardin and Stubbs, Impressionists, 19th-20th century Scottish painting including McTaggart, the Glasgow Boys and Scottish Colourists, and contemporary art. The temporary exhibitions programme in the Print Gallery is largely drawn from the gallery's own collection of about 20,000 artists' prints. Permanent display of printmaking techniques. Sculpture courtyard.

HUNTERIAN MUSEUM

University of Glasgow, Glasgow G12 8QQ
Tel:(041) 330 4221

University of Glasgow

Open all year Mon-Fri 9.30-5 Sat 9.30-1 May-Oct
also Sat 9.30-5 Sun 2-5. Admission free.
PPA, ST, 50%, G, C

West end of city, parking nearby, coaches must book,
refreshments, sales area, temporary exhibitions, wc,
parties welcome but must book.

This university museum has twice been named
Scottish Museum of the Year for its exhibitions
of the history of the University since 1451 and
its coin gallery. It also contains displays of
prehistoric and Roman archaeology,
ethnography with important collections
brought back from the Pacific by Captain Cook,
minerals and important fossils including the
Bearsden shark, dinosaur footprints, and a
plesiosaurus skeleton. Extensive research
collections are available to scholars.

KELLY GALLERY

118 Douglas Street, Glasgow G2 4ET
Tel:(041) 248 6386
Correspondence to: Royal Glasgow Institute of the
Fine Arts, 12 Sandyford Place, Glasgow G3 7NE.

The Royal Glasgow Institute of the Fine Arts

Open Mon-Fri 10.30-2 & 2.30-5.30 Sat 10-12.30.
Admission free.
P, L, 100%, G

City centre, sales area, temporary exhibitions, parties
welcome no need to book.

Individual artists and groups lease this gallery
to show their own works. The result is a
fascinating programme of contemporary art
exhibitions.

McLELLAN GALLERIES

270 Sauchiehall Street, Glasgow G2 2EH
Tel:(041) 331 1854

City of Glasgow District Council

Open all year Mon-Wed,Fri,Sat 10-6 Thu 10-10 Sun
12-6. Admission charges (with concessions).
L, 100%, WC, G

City centre, parking nearby, temporary exhibitions,
wc.

The purpose-built 1854 exhibition galleries,
completely refurbished in time for Glasgow's
celebrations as European City of Culture 1990,
now provide Glasgow museums with a major
exhibition venue for large temporary
exhibitions. Contact Museum Education
Department (tel:(041) 357 3929) for details of
educational activities.

MITCHELL LIBRARY

North Street, Glasgow G3 7DN
Tel:(041) 221 7030

City of Glasgow District Council

Open all year Mon-Fri 9.30-9 Sat 9.30-5. Admission
free.
PPA, L, WC, G, C

Charing Cross, parking nearby, refreshments, sales
area, temporary exhibitions, wc, parties welcome but
must book.

This large library has been extended regularly
since its move to North Street in 1911, the
most recent addition being completed in 1981.
Regular exhibitions ranging from canals to
cameras, manuscripts to music are shown on
each of the 5 levels.

MUSEUM OF TRANSPORT

Kelvin Hall, 1 Bunhouse Road, Glasgow G3 8DP
Tel:(041) 357 3929

City of Glasgow District Council

Open all year Mon-Fri 10-5 Sat 10-10 Sun 12-6.
Admission free.
P, L, 100%, WC, G, C, AD

1 1/2 miles from the city centre off Pollokshaws Road
(A77), parking for cars, wc, parties welcome no need
to book.

Museum devoted to the history of transport on
land and sea with examples from the important
collections of the Technology Department,
including bicycles and motor-cycles, horse-
drawn vehicles, buses, trams, railway
locomotives, fire engines and cars, with some
working models. Thematic displays include
the Clyde Room of ship models and Kelvin
Street, with 1938 shop fronts and period
vehicles, also a reconstruction of Glasgow
Subway Merkland Street Station. Contact the
Museum Education Department (tel:(041) 334
1131) for details of educational services.

PEOPLE'S PALACE MUSEUM

Glasgow Green, Glasgow G40 1AT
Tel:(041) 554 0223

City of Glasgow District Council

Open all year Mon-Wed,Fri,Sat 10-5 Thu 10-10 Sun
12-6. Admission free.
P, R, <50%, WC, G

1/2 mile east of Glasgow Green off London Road,
parking for cars & coaches, sales area, temporary
exhibitions, wc, parties welcome but must book.

Opened in 1898 for the working classes, this is Glasgow's social history museum. Collections from 1175 to the present day relate to trade, industry and Glasgow institutions, social, political and religious movements including temperance, franchise extension, co-operation, women's suffrage and socialism. Public art (Glasgow stained glass and tiles) and exhibits on popular culture, including football, cycling, theatre and cinema are also displayed in this fascinating museum. There is a wholefood snack bar in the Winter Gardens, the adjacent large glasshouse. Contact the Museum Education Department (tel:(041) 334 1131) for details of educational services.

POLLOK HOUSE

2060 Pollokshaws Road, Pollok Country Park, Glasgow G43 1AT
Tel:(041) 632 0274

City of Glasgow District Council

Open all year Mon,Tue,Thu-Sat 10-5 Wed 10-10 Sun 12-6. Admission free.
PPA, R, <50%, G, C, AD

South side of city in park, parking for cars & coaches, refreshments, sales area, temporary exhibitions, wc, parties welcome but must book.

Sharing parkland with the Burrell Collection, this house was built c.1750 with Edwardian additions to the design of Sir Robert Anderson. The house contains the Stirling Maxwell Collection of Spanish and other European paintings, furniture, ceramics and silver mostly of the late 18th and early 19th centuries. There is a picnic area and occasional evening events are held. Contact the Museum Education Department (tel:(041) 334 1131) for details of educational activities.

PROVAND'S LORDSHIP

3 Castle Street, Glasgow G4 0RB
Tel:(041) 552 8819

City of Glasgow District Council

Open all year Mon-Sat 10-5 Sun 2-5. Admission free.
<50%, G

Opposite Glasgow Cathedral near the city centre, parking for cars, sales area, temporary exhibitions, parties welcome but must book.

Facing the cathedral, the only other surviving medieval building in Glasgow, the Provand's Lordship was built in 1471. Period room displays range in date from 1500 to 1918.

ROYAL HIGHLAND FUSILIERS REGIMENTAL MUSEUM

518 Sauchiehall Street, Glasgow G2 3LW
Tel:(041) 332 0961

The Regiment

Open all year Mon-Thu 9-4.30 Fri 9-4. Admission free.
PPA, L/R, 100%, H, G

East of Charing Cross, sales area, parties welcome but must book.

Medals, uniforms, regimental silver, photographs and various other pieces of militaria tell the history of the Royal Highland Fusiliers from 1678 to the present day.

SCOTLAND STREET SCHOOL MUSEUM OF EDUCATION

225 Scotland Street, Glasgow G5 8QB
Tel:(041) 429 1202

Strathclyde Regional Council

Opening after September 1990, Mon-Sat 10-5, Sun 2-5. Admission free.
P, R, <50%, WC, G, C

Opposite Shields Road underground station, parking for cars & coaches, refreshments sales area, wc.

This re-creation of turn-of-the-century schooldays is housed in a former school designed by Charles Rennie Mackintosh.

SPRINGBURN MUSEUM

Atlas Square, Ayr Street, Springburn, Glasgow G21 4BW
Tel:(041) 557 1405

Springburn Museum Trust

Open all year Mon-Fri 10.30-5 Sat 10-4.30 Sun 2-5. Admission free.
R, 100%, G

2 miles north of Glasgow city centre on A803, direct train service to Springburn, parking for cars & coaches, sales area, temporary exhibitions, wc, parties welcome, booking preferred.

Springburn Museum is Glasgow's first community museum. Its constantly changing temporary exhibitions tell the story of community life past and present in what was once the largest centre of steam locomotive manufacture in Europe. Winner of the British Museum of the Year Award for social and industrial history in 1989.

THE TENEMENT HOUSE

145 Buccleuch Street, Glasgow G3
Tel:(041) 333 0183

National Trust for Scotland

Open Apr-Oct daily 2-5 Nov-Mar Sat,Sun 2-4. Last admission 1/2 hour before closing. Groups at other times by appointment. Admission charges (with concessions).
ST, G

Near Charing Cross tube station, parties welcome but must book (12 max).

Built in 1892 when Garnethill was a superior residential district in Glasgow's west end, the Tenement House illustrates life in the city at the turn of the century. The flat consists of two rooms, kitchen and bathroom, furnished with the everyday objects of that period. Another flat on the ground floor provides reception, interpretive and educational facilities.

THIRD EYE CENTRE

350 Sauchiehall Street, Glasgow G2 3JD
Tel:(041) 332 7521

Third Eye Centre (Glasgow) Ltd.

Open all year Tue-Sat 10-10 Sun 12-5.30. For evening events see current publicity. Admission free.
PPA, L, 100%, WC, G, C, B, AD

Near city centre, refreshments, sales area, temporary exhibitions, wc, parties welcome but must book.

Third Eye Centre is the main multi-purpose arts centre in Scotland. It promotes the visual arts through an extensive programme of new exhibitions and also promotes the performing arts through daytime and evening entertainment. As well as gallery space the building contains a shop, two studio theatres, cafe, bar and publishing house.

GLENFINNAN

GLENFINNAN MONUMENT & VISITOR CENTRE

Glenfinnan, Inverness-shire PH37 4LT
Tel:(039 783) 250

National Trust for Scotland

Open Easter-Jun & Sep-Oct daily 10-5.30 Jul-Aug daily 9-6.30. Admission charges (with concessions).
P, L/ST, G, C

18 miles west of Fort William on A830, parking for cars & coaches, refreshments, sales area, wc, parties welcome booking preferred.

The 65 foot pillar surmounted by a Highlander was erected in 1815 in tribute to the Clansmen who fought and died in the cause of Bonnie Prince Charlie. The Glenfinnan Games are held in August.

GREENOCK

McLEAN MUSEUM & ART GALLERY

5 Kelly Street, Greenock PA16 8JX
Tel:(0475) 23741

Inverclyde District Council

Open all year Mon-Sat 10-12 & 1-5. Admission free.
R, <50%, G

West side of Greenock, parking for cars, sales area, temporary exhibitions, wc, parties welcome but must book.

The museum displays material relating to many aspects of the social, industrial and maritime history of Inverclyde District. There is also an important collection of paintings by Scottish artists, ethnographic material and exhibits of natural history.

HAMILTON

THE CAMERONIANS' (SCOTTISH RIFLES) REGIMENTAL MUSEUM

Mote Hill, off Muir Street, Hamilton ML3 8BJ
Tel:(0698) 428688

Regimental Trustees

Open all year Fri-Wed 10-1 & 2-5. Admission free.
P, ST, 100%, G, AD

Adjacent to park, parking for cars & coaches, sales area, wc, parties welcome but must book.

Mementoes, relics, uniforms, medals and photographs, telling the history of the regiment from 1689 to the present. Strathclyde Country Park is suitable for picnics and offers a wide range of leisure activities during the summer months.

HAMILTON DISTRICT MUSEUM

129 Muir Street, Hamilton, Lanarkshire ML3 6BJ
Tel:(0698) 283981

Hamilton District Council

Open all year Mon,Tue,Thu,Fri 10-5 Wed,Sat 10-12 & 1-5. Admission free.
ST, 50%, G

Town centre, parking for cars & coaches, sales area, temporary exhibitions, wc, parties welcome but must book.

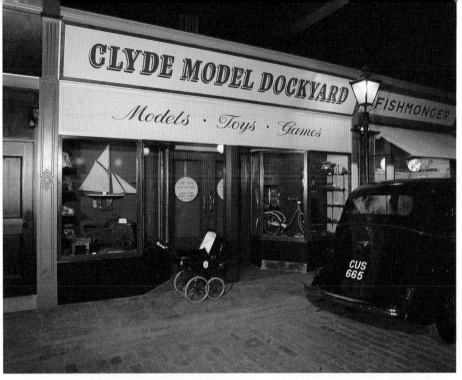

Museum of Transport: Kelvin Street with toy shop and fish shop. [*Glasgow Museums and Art Gallery*]

Museum of Transport: motor cycle display. [*Glasgow Museums and Art Gallery*]

Reconstruction of the 'single end' where David Livingstone was born. The David Livingstone Centre is housed in the tenements in Blantyre where the famous explorer spent his childhood.
[*Antonia Reeve/Scottish Museums Council*]

This museum is housed in a 17th century coaching inn with 18th century additions. The 18th century assembly room, complete with original plasterwork and musicians' gallery, is among the many unusual features of this, the oldest building in the town. Displays illustrate the history of Hamilton and environs with collections of period costume, 19th and early 20th century photographs, agricultural tools and implements and a reconstructed Victorian kitchen. Lacemaking, handloom weaving, coal-mining, archaeology and transport are described and illustrated in the permanent displays. There are varied temporary exhibition and educational programmes.

HELENSBURGH

THE HILL HOUSE

Upper Colquhoun Street, Helensburgh, Dunbartonshire
Tel:(0436) 3900

National Trust for Scotland

Open all year daily 1-5. Last admission 4.30. Admission charges (with concessions).
ST, G

23 miles north west of Glasgow off A814/B832, parking for cars & coaches, sales area, parties welcome but must book.

The Hill House is considered the finest example of the domestic architecture of Charles Rennie Mackintosh. It was commissioned by Walter Blackie, the Glasgow publisher, as his family residence in 1902. There is an exhibition on the life of Mackintosh.

HYNISH

SKERRYVORE MUSEUM

Hynish, Isle of Tiree, Argyll
Curator L. MacFarlane Tel:(08792) 691.

Hebridean Trust

Open daily 9-6. Admission free.
L/R/ST, <50%, G

On island, parking for cars & coaches, not suitable for large parties.

The museum tells the story of the building of the Skerryvore Lighthouse, 12 miles to the south west of the Isle of Tiree. The lighthouse may be viewed by telescope. A unique fresh water flushing harbour and pier is being restored by the Trust.

INVERARAY

AUCHINDRAIN MUSEUM OF COUNTRY LIFE

Inveraray, Argyll PA32 8XN
Tel:(049 95) 235

Auchindrain Museum Trust

Open Good Fri-Sep Sun-Fri 11-4 Jun,Jul,Aug daily 10-5. Admission charges.
ST, 100%, G

5 miles west of Inveraray on A83, parking for cars & coaches, sales area, wc, parties welcome no need to book.

Auchindrain is the only communal tenancy West Highland farming township to have survived in much of its original form. The buildings have been restored and are furnished in period styles to convey the life of the Highlands in past centuries.

INVERARAY BELL TOWER

All Saint's Episcopal Church, The Avenue, Inveraray, Argyll
Correspondence to Mr. N. Chaddock, 'Tighcladich', St.Catherine's, Argyll PA25 8AZ. Tel:(0499) 2433.

Scottish Episcopal Church

Open early May-late Sep Mon-Sat 10-1 & 2-5 Sun 2-5. Admission charges (with concessions).
P, ST, 50%, G

In town, parking for cars & coaches, sales area, temporary exhibitions, parties welcome no need to book.

The 126ft tower was built by the 10th Duke of Argyll in the fulfilment of a lifelong ambition. It contains a fine ring of ten bells and is set in pleasant grounds. Exhibitions of vestments and campanology on the ground floor and excellent views from the bell-tower. Phone for details of bell-ringing times. Recordings of bells and chimes can be heard whenever the tower is open.

INVERARAY CASTLE

Argyll Estates Office, Cherry Park, Inveraray, Argyll PA32 8XE
Tel:(0499) 2203

Trustees of the Tenth Duke of Argyll

Open Apr-Oct Mon-Thu & Sat 10-1 & 2-6 Sun 1-6 Jul,Aug Mon-Sat 10-6 Sun 1-6. Last admission 1/2 hour before closing. Admission charges (with concessions).
ST, G, C

1/2 mile north of Inveraray, parking for cars & coaches, refreshments, sales area, wc, parties welcome but must book.

A typical example of gothic revival in Britain, Inveraray Castle, the home of the Duke and Duchess of Argyll, was erected between 1740 and 1790. It contains a fine collection of tapestries, arms and armour, 18th century furniture, paintings and china. The armoury hall alone contains approximately 1300 pieces. Special arrangements can be made for school parties.

INVERARAY JAIL

Inveraray, Argyll PA32 8TX
Tel:(0499) 2381

Private

Open daily all year summer 9.30-6 winter 10-5. Last admission 1 hour before closing. Admission charges (with concessions).
PPA, L/R, <50%, WC, G

Town centre, parking nearby, sales area, wc, parties welcome booking preferred.

A reconstruction of life in a 19th century Scottish prison. Costumed interpreters, re-enacted trials, and furnished cells with authentic sounds and smells bring the Courthouse and County Prisons of Argyll back to life.

IONA

IONA ABBEY MUSEUM

The Abbey, Iona, Argyll PA76 6SN
Tel:(068 17) 404

Trustees of Iona Abbey

Open daily 9-6. Admission free.
L/R, 100%, G, C

Beside Abbey, no cars permitted on island, refreshments, sales area, wc.

The Abbey Museum has a unique collection of Celtic gravestones and crosses including St Columba's 'pillow cross'. The Benedictine Abbey is architecturally interesting, with parts dating from the 13th century. Guided tours of the Abbey are available.

IRVINE

GLASGOW VENNEL MUSEUM AND BURNS' HECKLING SHOP

4 & 10 Glasgow Vennel, Irvine, Ayrshire KA12 0BD.
Tel:(0294) 75059

Cunninghame District Council

Open Jun-Sep Mon-Tue & Thu-Sat 10-1 & 2-5 Sun 2-5 Oct-May Tue, Thu-Sat 10-1 & 2-5. Admission free.

P, L/ST, 50%, G

Near town centre, temporary exhibitions, wc.

No. 4 The Vennel holds a reconstruction of Burns' bedroom as it was in 1781. It shows the harsh conditions in which he lived while working in the Heckling Shop. The Heckling Shop is one of the few thatched buildings left in South-West Scotland. No. 10 is an intimate gallery which shows a varied exhibition programme throughout the year, including the work of local groups.

IRVINE BURNS CLUB MUSEUM & BURGH OF IRVINE MUSEUM

Wellwood, Eglinton Street, Irvine, Ayrshire
Tel:(0294) 74511
Correspondence to S K Gaw, Secretary, Camasunary, Kidsneuk, Irvine KA12 8SR. Tel:(0294) 79056.

Irvine Burns Club

Open all year Sat 2.30-5. Other times by appointment. Admission free.
P, ST, 50%, G, C, B, AD

Town centre, parking for cars & coaches, sales area, temporary exhibitions, wc, parties welcome but must book.

The Burns Club was founded in 1826 by friends of Robert Burns. Its museum contains manuscripts of the first edition of the poems and other Burnsiana. One room contains displays on Burns' work as a flax dresser. Letters from Honorary Members of the Club such as Dickens, Garibaldi and Tennyson are on display. Displays devoted to the history of the Royal Burgh of Irvine include muniments.

SCOTTISH MARITIME MUSEUM

Laird Forge, Gottries Road, Irvine KA12 8QE
Tel:(0294) 78283

Scottish Maritime Museum Trust

Open mid Apr-Oct daily 10-4.30. Admission charges (with concessions).
R, 100%, G

Irvine harbourside, refreshments, sales area, temporary exhibitions, parties welcome but must book.

This unique museum is conceived as a living, working environment in which visitors can witness traditional maritime skills and handle for themselves the equipment and tools used on shore and at sea. Boats on display include a Puffer 'Spartan' and a tug 'Garnock'. The quayside exhibition area has a recreated working class family flat and an operating boat slip. Special events and demonstration days held regularly.

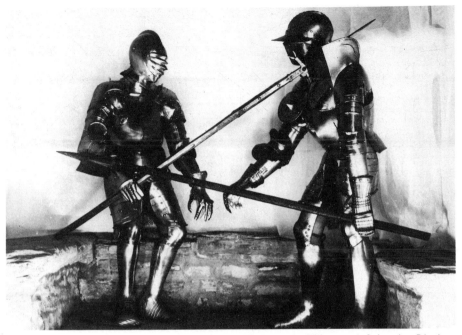

26   Arms and armour on display at Dean Castle, Kilmarnock. *[Kilmarnock & Loudon District Museums]*

ISLE OF ISLAY

FINLAGGAN

Isle of Islay
Correspondence to Donald Bell, The Cottage, Bally Grant, Islay. Tel:(04714) 275.

Finlaggan Trust

Open summer daylight hours. Admission free.

Loch shore.

Finlaggan is known as the 'Cradle of Clan Donald', and Chiefs of the clan lived there from the 12th to the 16th centuries. Archaeological finds on display in a farm cottage on the shores of the loch indicate the importance of this site. There is a display on the crowning ceremony of the Lords of the Isles.

MUSEUM OF ISLAY LIFE

Port Charlotte, Isle of Islay, Argyll PA48 7UA
Tel:(049 685) 358

Islay Museums Trust

Open Mar-Oct Mon-Sat 10-5 Sun 2-5 Nov,Jan,Feb Mon-Fri 10-4.30 Sun 2-4. Admission charges (with concessions).
P, ST, 100%, G

In old church off A847, parking for cars & coaches, sales area, wc, parties welcome but must book.

Part of the museum is devoted to Victorian domestic items, attractively displayed in two room settings, a bedroom and a kitchen. Industry is represented by displays of whisky making, including an 'illicit' still, wheelwrights', coopers' and leather workers' tools, a selection of hand agricultural implements and much more. An important collection of carved stones dating from the 6th to the 16th century is housed in the lapidarium below the museum. There is an extensive reference library of material on Islay.

KILBARCHAN

WEAVER'S COTTAGE

Kilbarchan, Renfrewshire
Tel:(05057) 5588

National Trust for Scotland

Open Apr-May & Sep-Oct Tue,Thu,Sat,Sun 2-5 Jun-Aug daily 2-5. Admission charges (with concessions).
ST, G

8 miles south west of Glasgow off A737, parking for cars & coaches, parties welcome but must book.

Furnished as an 18th century weaver's cottage with handlooms, various pieces of weaving equipment and typical domestic utensils. Check times for weaving demonstrations.

KILMARNOCK

DEAN CASTLE

Dean Road, Kilmarnock KA3 1XB
Correspondence to Curator, Dick Institute, Elmbank Avenue, Kilmarnock KA1 3BU. Tel:(0563) 22700 or 26401.

Kilmarnock & Loudoun District Council

Open daily 12-5. Groups at other times by appointment. Admission charges (with concessions). P, R/ST, <50%, WC, G, C

On north side of town off A77, parking for cars & coaches, refreshments, sales area, temporary exhibitions, wc, parties welcome but must book.

A splendid example of 14th and 15th century architecture, this castle contains a fine collection of European arms and armour, early European musical instruments and tapestries. It is set in a country park with nature trail and other walks.

DICK INSTITUTE

Elmbank Avenue, Kilmarnock KA1 3BU
Tel:(0563) 26401 ex.36

Kilmarnock & Loudoun District Council

Open all year summer Mon,Tue,Thu,Fri 10-8 Wed & Sat 10-5 winter Mon,Tue,Thu,Fri 10-5 Wed & Sat 10-5. Admission free.
P, R, 100%, WC, G, AD

1/4 mile from town centre on A71, parking for cars & coaches, sales area, temporary exhibitions, wc, parties welcome but must book.

The art gallery has been modernised recently to a high standard. Temporary exhibitions (touring and collection) change frequently. The museum contains interesting collections of shells, small arms, ethnography and Scottish archaeological specimens and fossils of international importance. The library contains books on Ayrshire and by Burns.

KILMAURS

KILMAURS HISTORICAL SOCIETY MUSEUM

13 Irvine Road, Kilmaurs, Ayrshire KA3 2RJ
Correspondence to Secretary, Mr Beattie, 34 East Park Crescent, Kilmaurs, Ayrshire KA3 2QT.

Kilmaurs Historical Society

Open summer Wed,Sat,Sun afternoons. Other times by appointment. Admission free.
P, ST, 100%, G

Centre of Kilmaurs off A735, wc, parties welcome but must book.

Local history museum in former village school containing Free Gardeners' regalia, banners and agricultural equipment, particularly relating to dairy farming. There is an 18 ft. model of the old Railway Station.

KILSYTH

COLZIUM MUSEUM AND GROUNDS

Colzium-Lennox Estate, Kilsyth G65 0RZ
Contact District Museums Service. Tel:(0236) 735077.

Cumbernauld & Kilsyth District Council

Open all year House Sun-Sat 10-5. Museum Wed 2-8. Admission free.
P, L/R, ST, <50%, G

1 mile east of Kilsyth on A803, parking for cars & coaches, refreshments, wc, parties welcome but must book.

The house contains a recently refurbished museum and art gallery. The museum illustrates the history of Kilsyth and the Colzium area, and the Battle of Kilsyth. The grounds contain a walled garden, children's zoo and woodland walks.

KILSYTH'S HERITAGE MUSEUM

Kilsyth Library, Burngreen, Kilsyth
Tel:(0236) 823147

Cumbernauld & Kilsyth District Council

Open all year Mon, Wed, Fri 9.30-1 & 2.30-7 Tue 9.30-1 & 2-5 Thu 9.30-1 Sat 9-12. Admission free.
ST, <50%, G

East of town centre off A803, parking for cars & coaches, sales area.

This small local museum illustrates the history of Kilsyth from the 18th century to the present.

KIRKINTILLOCH

AULD KIRK MUSEUM

The Cowgate, Kirkintilloch, Glasgow G66 1AB
Correspondence to Strathkelvin District Museums, The Cross, Kirkintilloch, Glasgow G66 1PW.
Tel:(041) 775 1185.

Strathkelvin District Council

Open all year Tue,Thu,Fri 2-5 Sat 10-1 & 2-5. Admission free.
50%

Town centre, parking for cars & coaches, temporary exhibitions, wc, parties welcome but must book.

This museum is housed in one of the oldest buildings still standing in Kirkintilloch, constructed in 1644. Exhibitions ranging from local history to photography and art are held regularly throughout the year. See Barony Chambers Museum for details of education service.

BARONY CHAMBERS MUSEUM

The Cross, Kirkintilloch, Glasgow G66 1AB
Correspondence to Strathkelvin District Museums,
The Cross, Kirkintilloch, Glasgow G66 1PW.
Tel:(041) 775 1185.

Strathkelvin District Council

Open all year Tue,Thu,Fri 2-5 Sat 10-1 & 2-5.
Admission free.
ST, 50%

Town centre, parking for cars & coaches, sales area,
parties welcome but must book.

Throughout its history Barony Chambers has
been at different times a town hall, council
chambers and court room, jail and school. Now
a museum, opened in 1982, it illustrates the
social and industrial history of the Kirkintilloch
district. A reconstructed 'single end' and wash-
house give a vivid picture of early 20th century
working class life. Iron founding, coal mining,
weaving and boat building are described in
displays of photographs, tools and equipment.
There are also displays on the Forth and
Clyde Canal. Classes, special activities and
worksheets can be provided for schools and
museum staff are available for school visits.

KIRKOSWALD

SOUTER JOHNNIE'S COTTAGE

Main Street, Kirkoswald, Ayrshire
Tel:(065 56) 603 or 274

National Trust for Scotland

Open Apr-Oct daily 12-5. Other times by
appointment. Admission charges (with concessions).
P, ST, G

4 miles west of Maybole on A77, parking nearby,
parties welcome but must book.

Associated with the souter (cobbler) in Burns'
poem 'Tam O'Shanter', this thatched cottage
displays Burns' relics, an interesting collection
of cobbler's tools and life-size stone figures in
a reconstructed ale-house.

LANGBANK

FINLAYSTONE DOLL COLLECTION

Finlaystone, Langbank, Renfrewshire PA14 6TJ
Tel:(047 554) 285

Mrs. Jane MacMillan

Open Apr-Aug Sun 2.30-4.30. Other times by
appointment. Admission charges.
P, L, 100%, WC, G, C, AD, SL

West of Glasgow & Langbank on A8, parking for
cars & coaches, temporary exhibitions, wc, parties
welcome but must book.

A collection of over 600 dolls of all ages and
many nationalities, many displayed in a historic
house. Refreshments are available in the
summer months. Also interesting woods and
gardens with visitor centre and play area open
all year.

LARGS

KIRKGATE HOUSE

Manse Court, Largs KA30 8AW
Tel:(0475) 687081

Largs & District Historical Society

Open Jun-Sep Mon-Sat 2-5. Other times by
appointment. Admission free.
P, ST, 100%, G

Town centre, sales area, temporary exhibitions, not
suitable for parties.

Once the home of the Brisbanes, Largs has
strong Australian connections. This small local
history museum contains books and
photographs relating to the family. It also
contains curling memorabilia from the
collection of Dr. Cairnie. A complete record
of graves in the old churchyard nearby is kept
at the museum.

LOCHWINNOCH

LOCHWINNOCH COMMUNITY MUSEUM

Main Street, Lochwinnoch
Tel:(0505) 842615

Renfrew District Council

Open all year Mon,Wed,Fri 10-1 & 2-5 & 6-8 Tue &
Sat 10-1 & 2-5. Admission free.
P, L, 100%, G

8 miles south west of Paisley on A737, parking for
cars, temporary exhibitions, parties welcome but
must book.

Opened in 1984 this new community museum
features a series of changing exhibitions which
describe the historic background of local
agriculture, industry and village life. There are
occasional special exhibitions.

MAUCHLINE

BURNS' HOUSE MUSEUM

Castle Street, Mauchline, Ayrshire
Tel:(0290) 50045

Burns' House Museum Committee

Open Easter-Sep Mon-Sat 11-12.30 & 2-5.30 Sun 2-5. Other times by appointment. Admission charges.
ST, 50%, AD

Town centre, parking nearby, sales area, wc, parties welcome but must book.

Robert Burns once lived in this house. As well as artefacts belonging to the poet, there is a fascinating collection of Mauchline box ware for which the town was famous in the 19th century. There is also a display on curling and curling stones relating to the local factory. A number of Burns' contemporaries including 'Holy Willie', Gavin Hamilton and 'Poosie Nansie' are buried in Mauchline Kirkyard opposite the museum.

MAYBOLE

CULZEAN CASTLE & COUNTRY PARK

Maybole, Ayrshire
Tel:(065 56) 269 or 274

National Trust for Scotland

Castle open May-Aug daily 10-6 Oct 10-6 Apr,Sep,Oct 12-5. Last admission 1/2 hour before closing. Country park all year 9-sunset. Admission charges (with concessions).
P, WC, H, C

12 miles south of Ayr on A719 & 4 miles west of Maybole, parking for cars & coaches, refreshments, sales area, temporary exhibitions, wc, parties welcome but must book.

This important Adam house with magnificent interior has been carefully restored to its original appearance and furnished appropriately. Contains an exhibition of early yachting and ship models and a display relating to General Eisenhower and his connections with Culzean. The farm buildings contain a display on the history of the estate. Magnificent country park with cliffs and rugged shore, woodlands, walled garden, deer park, nature walks, swan pond and fountain court.

MILLPORT

MUSEUM OF THE CUMBRAES

Garrison House, Millport, Isle of Cumbrae
Tel:(0475) 530741

Correspondence to District Curator, Cunninghame District Council Museums Service, 10 Glasgow Vennel, Irvine, KA12 0BD.

Cunninghame District Council

Open Jun-Sep Tue-Sat 10-4.30. Admission free.
R, 100%

Town centre, parking nearby, parties welcome no need to book.

A small local museum displaying the unique life of the Cumbrae Island. Exhibits include old photographs, local regalia and a reconstructed wash house.

ROBERTSON MUSEUM & AQUARIUM

University Marine Biological Station, Millport, Isle of Cumbrae
Tel:(047 553) 581

Universities of London & Glasgow

Open all year Mon-Fri 9.30-12.30 & 2-5 Apr-Sep also Sat 9.30-12.30 Easter & Jun-Sep also Sat 2-5. Admission charges.
PPA, R, 100%, G

Temporary exhibitions, wc, parties welcome but must book.

Devoted to exhibits on fisheries & marine science, this museum is housed in the oldest marine station in Britain.

MILNGAVIE

LILLIE ART GALLERY

Station Road, Milngavie, Glasgow
Tel:(041) 956 2351 weekends (041) 956 6350

Bearsden & Milngavie District Council

Open all year Tue-Fri 11-5 & 7-9 Sat & Sun 2-5. Admission free.
P, L/R/ST, 100%, G

Milngavie off A81 north of Glasgow centre, parking for cars & coaches, sales area, temporary exhibitions, wc, parties welcome no need to book.

Modern art gallery with a permanent collection of Scottish 20th century paintings which includes examples of work by the Glasgow Boys and Scottish Colourists. A selection from this collection is displayed regularly along with a continuous programme of temporary exhibitions. Regular evening events are held.

NEW LANARK

NEW LANARK

New Lanark Mills, New Lanark, Lanark ML11 9DB
Tel:(0555) 61345

New Lanark Conservation Trust

Village open at all times. Visitor Centre open daily 11-5. Admission charges (with concessions).
P, L, 100%, WC, G, C

1 mile south of Lanark off A70, parking for cars & coaches, refreshments, sales area, temporary exhibitions, wc, parties welcome but must book.

This 200 year old cotton spinning village is being restored and brought back to life. Founded by David Dale, the village became internationally famous when social reformer Robert Owen became managing partner in 1800. He spent 25 years in New Lanark, putting his social and environmental theories into practice. The Visitor Centre contains innovative exhibitions using laser and hologram technology, as well as working 19th century spinning machinery. The village also offers a Scottish Wildlife Trust Visitor Centre and picnic and play areas. School visits welcome.

OBAN

McCAIG MUSEUM

Corran Halls, Oban, Argyll
Correspondence to Branch Librarian, Oban Library, Corran Halls, Oban. Tel:(0631) 64211 ex 221.

Argyll & Bute District Council

Open all year Wed-Sat & Mon 10-1 & 2-5.30. Admission free.
R/ST, 100%, G

In town, parking for cars & coaches, refreshments, temporary exhibitions, wc, not suitable for parties.

Permanent displays of local, social and natural history.

PAISLEY

COATS OBSERVATORY

Oakshaw Street, Paisley, Renfrewshire
Tel:(041) 889 2013

Renfrew District Council

Open Mon,Tue,Thu 2-8 Wed,Fri,Sat 10-5. Admission free.
ST, G

Towards west end of town centre behind Paisley Museum, parties welcome but must book.

The tradition of astronomical observation and meteorological recording has continued since the observatory was built in 1882. The seismic equipment has been updated recently and the installation of a satellite weather picture receiver has made it one of the best equipped observatories in the country.

PAISLEY MUSEUM & ART GALLERY

High Street, Paisley PA1 2BA
Tel:(041) 889 3151

Renfrew District Council

Open all year Mon-Sat 10-5. Admission free.
PPA, ST, <50%, G

Towards west end of town centre, sales area, temporary exhibitions, parties welcome but must book.

This late 19th century museum and art gallery houses the world famous collection of Paisley shawls. Displays trace the history of the Paisley Pattern, the development of weaving techniques and the social aspects of what was a tight-knit weaving community. Also fine collections of local history, natural history, ceramics and Scottish paintings.

ROTHESAY

BUTE MUSEUM

Stuart Street, Rothesay, Isle of Bute
Tel: Hon. Secretary (0700) 2248.

Buteshire Natural History Society

Open all year Oct-Mar Tue-Sat 2.30-4.30 Apr-Sep Mon-Sat 10.30-12.30 & 2.30-4.30 mid Jun-Sep also Sun 2.30-4.30. Admission charges (with concessions).
ST, 100%, G

Town centre 5 mins from Rothesay Pier, parking for cars, sales area, temporary exhibitions, wc, parties welcome no need to book.

An island museum with local exhibits of natural and social history, including models of Clyde steamers and a collection of early Christian crosses. The archaeological section contains some significant finds from the Bronze and Iron Ages and tools and domestic items from recently excavated Neolithic burial cairns.

WINTER GARDEN

Argyll Street, Rothesay, Isle of Bute
Tel:(0700) 2487

Winter Garden Trust

Open daily 9-5 from June 1990. Admission charges (with concessions).
R, 100%, WC, G, C, B

In town, parking nearby, refreshments, sales area, wc, parties welcome booking preferred.

Rothesay's unique Winter Garden, meticulously restored to its original splendour, now houses an exhibition on the history of the island. Special emphasis is given to the role of Rothesay as one of Clydeside's most popular holiday resorts, with working displays by local craftsmen complemented by an audio-visual presentation on the journey and life 'doon the watter'.

RUTHERGLEN

RUTHERGLEN MUSEUM

King Street, Rutherglen G73 1DQ
Tel:(041) 647 0837

City of Glasgow District Council

Open all year Mon-Sat 10-5 Sun 2-5. Admission free.
P, L, 100%, G

In town, parking for cars, sales area, temporary exhibitions, wc, parties welcome but must book.

A museum of the history of the former Royal Burgh of Rutherglen, housed in the Burgh Court building. Collections include an extensive photographic record of the Burgh from 1860.

SALTCOATS

NORTH AYRSHIRE MUSEUM

Manse Street, Kirkgate, Saltcoats, Ayrshire
Tel:(0294) 64174
Correspondence to District Curator, Cunninghame District Museums Service, 10 Glasgow Vennel, Irvine KA12 0BD.

Cunninghame District Council

Open Jun-Sep Mon,Tue,Thu,Sat 10-1 & 2-5 Oct-May Tue,Thu,Sat 10-1 & 2-5. Admission free.
PPA, R, 100%, WC, G

Town centre, parking for cars, temporary exhibitions, wc, parties welcome no need to book.

This former local parish church is a good example of mid-18th century Scottish architecture. Displays reflect the life and work of the people of North Ayrshire. There is an active and changing exhibitions programme.

STEWARTON

STEWARTON & DISTRICT MUSEUM

District Council Chambers, Avenue Square, Stewarton, Ayrshire
Correspondence to Chairman of Museum Trustees, 17 Grange Terrace, Kilmarnock KA1 2JR.

Stewarton & District Historical Society

Open by appointment. Tel (0563) 24748 or (0560) 84249. Admission free.
P, ST, G

Town centre, parking for cars & coaches, wc, parties welcome but must book.

A small local history museum exhibiting items relating to church history, bonnet-making and the town's bonnet guild, as well as photographs and other records.

STRATHAVEN

JOHN HASTIE MUSEUM

Threestanes Road, Strathaven ML10 6DX
Tel:(0357) 21257
Correspondence to Chief Librarian, East Kilbride District Council, Central Library, The Olympia Centre, East Kilbride G74 1PG.

East Kilbride District Council

Open Apr-Sep Mon,Tue,Wed,Fri 2-5 Thu 2-4.30 Sat 11-1 & 2-5. Admission free.
P, ST, 50%, G

Junction off A71 & A726 in John Hastie Park, parking nearby, wc, parties welcome no need to book.

A local history museum with an impressive collection of pottery and porcelain including Wedgwood, Minton and Doulton. As Strathaven was at one time the home of a thriving community of handloom weavers there is a display of artefacts connected with weaving and associated crafts. Covenanting objects include a broadsword and a flag of French silk.

TARBOLTON

BACHELORS' CLUB

Sandgate, Tarbolton, Ayrshire
Tel:(0292) 541424

National Trust for Scotland

Open · Apr-Oct daily 12-5. Other times by appointment. Admission charges (with concessions).
L, 50%, G

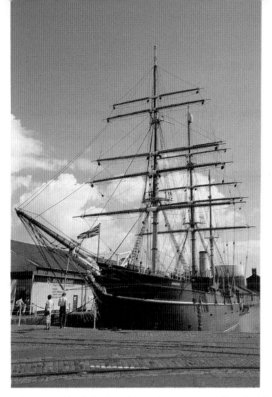

Royal Research Ship *Discovery*, built in Dundee and now returned to the Victoria Dock there. The ship is being restored by Dundee Heritage Trust. [*Dundee Heritage Trust*]

Mural commissioned by Dundee Museums and Art Galleries from local students, as part of the archaeology display in the McManus Galleries. [*The City of Dundee Art Galleries and Museums*]

Blair Castle, Blair Atholl, home of the 10th Duke of Atholl. One of the most striking and beautifully situated castles in the Scottish Baronial style. [*His Grace the Duke of Atholl*]

Signpost to the Museum at Shawbost where local schoolchildren have assembled objects relating to crofting, fishing and domestic life in Lewis. [*Eolas Photography*]

27   The kitchen/parlour of Bachelors' Club, Tarbolton. Period furnishings of the 1780s.
[National Trust for Scotland]

7 1/2 miles north east of Ayr off A758, parking for cars & coaches, sales area, parties welcome but must book.

The upstairs room in which Robert Burns was initiated into Freemasonry, attended dancing classes and helped found the Bachelors' Club debating society is furnished with period items and contains Burns' memorabilia. The lower room is set up as a typical cottage interior with a box bed.

TAYNUILT

BONAWE IRON WORKS

Taynuilt, Argyll
Tel:(031) 244 3101 for information.

Scottish Development Department (Historic Buildings and Monuments)

Open Apr-Sep Mon-Sat 9.30-7 Sun 2-7. Admission charges (with concessions).
P, L, G

Near Taynuilt village.

The mid-18th century charcoal-fuelled ironworks now houses displays on the iron-making process.

TOBERMORY

MULL MUSEUM

Main Street, Tobermory, Isle of Mull, Argyll PA75 6NY

Mull & Iona Museum Association

Open Apr-Sep Mon-Fri 10.30-4.30. Other times by arrangement. Admission charges.
P, L, 100%, G

Town centre, parking for cars & coaches, wc.

A small museum with collections relating to the island's past, including objects, photographs and documents. A reference library is available.

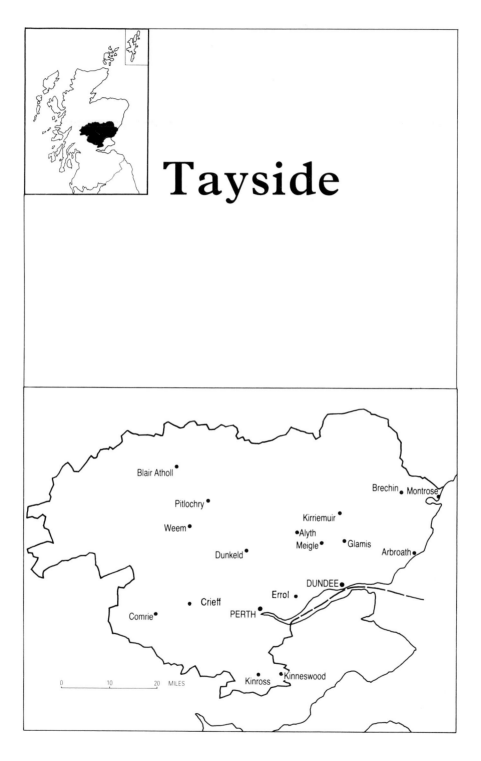

Tayside

ALYTH

ALYTH MUSEUM

Commercial Street, Alyth, Perthshire
Correspondence to Curator, Perth Museum & Art Gallery, George Street, Perth. Tel:(0738) 32488.

Perth & Kinross District Council

Open May-Sep Tue-Sat 1-5. Admission free.
ST, G

Alyth 19 miles from Perth off A93, parking nearby, not suitable for parties.

A small but interesting museum with domestic and rural material from the area.

ARBROATH

ARBROATH ABBEY

Arbroath, Angus
Tel:(031) 244 3101 for information.

Scottish Development Department (Historic Buildings and Monuments)

Open Jan-Mar & Oct-Dec Mon-Sat 9.30-4 Sun 2-4 Apr-Sep Mon-Sat 9.30-7 Sun 2-7. Admission charges (with concessions).
L, <50%, WC, G

Town centre.

The substantial ruins of a Tironensian monastery, including much of the abbey church and parts of the domestic buildings, notably the vaulted entrance and the abbot's house. The abbey is associated with the Declaration of Arbroath of 1320 which asserted Scotland's independence from England. The restored abbot's house contains a small display on the abbey and its history.

ARBROATH ART GALLERY

Public Library, Hill Terrace, Arbroath, Angus
Correspondence to Montrose Museum & Art Gallery, Panmure Place, Montrose DD10 8HE. Tel:(0674) 73232.

Angus District Council

Open all year Mon-Fri 9.30-6 Sat 9.30-5. Admission free.
PPA, ST, <50%, G

Town centre, parties welcome but must book.

An art gallery specialising in local work with a good collection of paintings by J.W. Herald, watercolourist. Two oils by Pieter Breughel also on display.

ARBROATH MUSEUM

Signal Tower, Ladyloan, Arbroath, Angus
Tel:(0674) 75598
Correspondence to Montrose Museum & Art Gallery, Panmure Place, Montrose DD10 8HE. Tel:(0674) 73232.

Angus District Council

Open Apr-Oct Mon-Sat 10.30-1 & 2-5 Jul-Aug also open Sun 2-5 Nov-Mar Mon-Fri 2-5 Sat 10.30-1 & 2-5. Admission free.
PPA, ST, 50%, G

Town centre, parking for cars, limited for coaches, sales area, wc, parties welcome but must book.

Housed in the signal tower to the Bell Rock Lighthouse built in 1813 by R. Stevenson, this local museum contains collections from prehistory to the industrial revolution. Displays include the Bell Rock Lighthouse, the fishing industry, local trades and wildlife.

ST. VIGEANS

Arbroath
Tel:(031) 244 3101 for information.

Scottish Development Department (Historic Buildings and Monuments)

Open all year Mon-Sat all reasonable times. Contact keyholder Mrs M Jamieson, 5 Kirkstyle, St Vigeans, Arbroath. Admission free.
G

1 1/2 miles north of Arbroath.

A fine collection of early Christian Pictish sculptured stones and medieval stonework from the original village church.

BLAIR ATHOLL

ATHOLL COUNTRY COLLECTION

The Old School, Blair Atholl, Perthshire PH18 5TT
Tel:(079 681) 232

Mr. & Mrs. J. Cameron

Open Easter, Jun-mid Oct daily 1.30-5.30 Jul-Sep also Mon-Fri 9.30-5.30. Other times by appointment. Admission charges.
P, R, 50%, WC, G

Town centre, parking for cars & coaches, sales area, wc, parties welcome but must book.

Turn in at the sign of the white horse. Exhibits tell the story of how the villagers and glen folk lived in years gone by and include a blacksmith's smiddy and a crofter's stable and byre. Displays describe flax growing and spinning, once important to this district. Road, rail and postal services, the school, the kirk, the vet and gamekeeper are all featured. Children may handle and touch many of the items.

28   A weaver's loom on display at the Scottish Tartans Museum, Comrie. *[Scottish Tartans Museum]*

BLAIR CASTLE

Blair Atholl, Pitlochry, Perthshire PH18 5TH
Tel:(079 681) 207

His Grace the Duke of Atholl

Open Apr-Oct Mon-Sat 10-6 Apr,May,Oct Sun 2-6 Jun-Sep 10-6. Last admission one hour before closing. Admission charges (with concessions).
P, L/ST, <50%, WC, G, C

7 miles north west of Pitlochry off A9, parking for cars & coaches, refreshments, sales area, temporary exhibitions, wc, parties welcome no need to book.

This original 13th century tower has additions in the Scottish baronial style. The castle contains charmingly furnished period rooms, Jacobite relics, needlework, lace, fine collections of firearms and militaria, china and masonic regalia. Other facilities include picnic areas, nature trails, pony trekking, deer park and a regular programme of special events.

CLAN DONNACHAIDH (ROBERTSON) MUSEUM

Bruar Falls, Blair Atholl, Perthshire
Tel:(079683) 264

Clan Donnachaidh Society

Open mid Apr-mid Oct Mon, Wed-Sat 10-5 Sun 2-5. Other times by appointment.

3 miles north west of Blair Atholl on A9, parking for cars & coaches, sales area, wc, parties welcome no need to book.

Documents, books and pictures associated with the Clan Donnachaidh (Robertsons, Reids, Duncans, and others). Contains the Stone of the Standard, 'Clan na Bratach', traditionally connected with the Battle of Bannockburn 1314.

BRECHIN

BRECHIN MUSEUM

St. Ninian's Square, Brechin, Angus
Correspondence to Montrose Museum & Art Gallery, Panmure Place, Montrose DD10 8HE. Tel:(0674) 73232.

Angus District Council

Open all year Mon,Tue,Thu,Fri 9.30-6 Wed 9.30-7 Sat 9.30-5. Admission free.
PPA, ST, G

Town centre, parking for cars & 2 coaches, wc, parties welcome but must book.

Local history collections feature the Burgh Regalia, church history, local archaeology and trades. Small display of works by David Waterson R.A., etcher and watercolourist.

COMRIE

SCOTTISH TARTANS MUSEUM

Davidson House, Drummond Street, Comrie, Perthshire PH6 2DW
Tel:(0764) 70779

Scottish Tartans Society

Open all year May-Sep Mon-Sat 10-5 Sun 11-3 Mar-Apr & Oct Mon-Fri 10-5 Sat 10-1 Nov-Feb Mon-Sat 10-1. Admission charges (with concessions).
P, L/R, 100%, G

Town centre, sales area, wc, parties welcome but must book.

Everything you ever wanted to know about the history and development of tartan and Highland dress. Plants used for natural dyeing are grown in a 'dye' garden at the museum. A research service is available to track down your tartan.

CRIEFF

HIGHLAND TRYST MUSEUM

Burrell Street, Crieff, Perthshire PH7 4DG
Tel:(0764) 5202

Highland Tryst Charitable Trust

Open all year Easter-Oct daily 9-6.30 Nov-Mar Mon-Sat 10-4.30. Admission charges.
P, R, 50%, WC, G, C

Town centre, on A822, parking for cars & coaches, refreshments sales area, wc, parties welcome no need to book.

This museum portrays the story of Crieff, capital of royal Strathearn, wild frontier town where Highlands met Lowlands, and the people who lived on that frontier. A handloom weaver making tartan cloth in the old weavers' house carries on a tradition of the town dating from at least the early 17th century.

DUNDEE

BARRACK STREET MUSEUM

Barrack Street, Dundee
Correspondence to McManus Galleries, Albert Square, Dundee DD1 1DA. Tel:(0382) 23141.

City of Dundee District Council

Open all year Mon-Sat 10-5. Admission free.
ST, <50%, G

Town centre, sales area, temporary exhibitions, wc, parties welcome but must book.

This branch museum contains displays on wildlife in Dundee and the geology and wildlife of Scotland. Exhibits include an observation bee-hive and skeleton of the Great Tay Whale. See McManus Galleries for details of schools programme and other activities.

BROUGHTY CASTLE MUSEUM

St. Vincent Street, Broughty Ferry, Dundee
Correspondence to McManus Galleries, Albert Square, Dundee DD1 1DA. Tel:(0382) 23141.

City of Dundee District Council

Open all year Mon-Thu & Sat 10-1 & 2-5 Jul-Sep also Sun 2-5. Admission free.

Five miles east of city centre on sea front, parking for cars & coaches, sales area, parties welcome but must book.

A reconstructed estuary fort now houses this local history museum. Exhibits relate to the maritime history of the area in particular whaling, fishing, the ferry and lifeboat services. Arms and armour are also on display. See McManus Galleries for details of schools programme and other activities.

DUNDEE PRINTMAKERS WORKSHOP / SEAGATE GALLERY

38-40 Seagate, Dundee DD1 2EJ
Tel:(0382) 26331

Management Committee

Open all year gallery Mon-Sat 10-5.30, workshop Mon-Thu 9.30-5 & 6.30-9.30 Fri 9.30-5 Sat 10-5 Sun 12-5. Admission free.
ST, 100%, WC, G

City centre, parking nearby, sales area, temporary exhibitions, wc, parties welcome no need to book.

This gallery and workshop promotes the contemporary visual arts through provision of printmaking facilities, editioning, workshops, educational classes, talks and demonstrations. A continuous programme of events and exhibitions with educational workshops operates throughout the year in the Seagate Gallery, and in addition there is a small print gallery offering a wide selection of members' work. There is a print hire scheme in operation.

FRANCIS COOPER & MATTHEW GALLERIES

Duncan of Jordonstone College of Art, Perth Road, Dundee DD1 4HT
Tel:(0382) 23261 ext. 291

Board of Governors

Open Oct-April Francis Cooper Mon-Fri 10-4, Matthew Mon-Thu 9.30-8.30 & Fri 9.30-5, Level 5 Artspace Matthew Building Mon-Fri 9-8.30 Sat 9-4. Admission free.
P, L/R, 100%, WC, G

15 minutes walk from BR station, parking nearby, refreshments, temporary exhibitions, wc, parties welcome no need to book.

International and British touring exhibitions relating to fine art, design, photography, video and architecture are held in these college galleries. A small permanent collection of fine art and design work is exhibited occasionally. The galleries are also open during the last two weeks in June for the annual exhibition of graduates' work.

H.M. FRIGATE 'UNICORN'

Victoria Dock, Dundee DD1 3JA
Tel:(0382) 200900

Unicorn Preservation Society

Open Apr-Oct Sun-Fri 10-5, Sat 10-4 mid Oct-Mar Mon-Fri 10-4. Admission charges (with concessions).
R, <50%

Berthed at Victoria Dock, parking for cars & coaches, sales area, wc, parties welcome no need to book.

The oldest British-built warship still afloat, 'HMS Unicorn' was launched in 1824. It portrays the flavour of life in the Royal Navy during the 'golden age' of sail.

McMANUS GALLERIES (formerly Central Museum & Art Gallery)

Albert Square, Dundee DD1 1DA
Tel:(0382) 23141

City of Dundee District Council

Open all year Mon-Sat 10-5. Admission free.
PPA, L, 100%, WC, G

Town centre, sales area, temporary exhibitions, wc, parties welcome booking preferred.

This finely restored Victorian gothic building by Gilbert Scott contains local history displays of trade and industry, social history and archaeology. Art galleries contain fine collections of Victorian and more recent Scottish paintings, sculpture, ceramics, glass. Regular programme of temporary exhibitions. For information on the active schools and community programme which includes lectures, visits, workshops, school and community loan service, publications, reminiscence groups, holiday activities, contact the museum education services department. Evening lectures and guided walks for adults are also organised.

MILLS OBSERVATORY

Balgay Park, Glamis Road, Dundee DD2 2UB
Tel:(0382) 67138

City of Dundee District Council

Open all year Apr-Sep Mon-Fri 10-5 Sat 2-5 Oct-Mar Mon-Fri 3-10 Sat 2-5. Admission free.
P, ST, 50%, G

One mile west of city centre, parking for cars, coaches at foot of hill, sales area, temporary exhibitions, wc, parties welcome but must book.

A museum with a difference contained within an active public observatory with a very fine Victorian 10in Cooke refracting telescope, ideal for viewing the moon and planets. There is an audio-visual show and displays on astronomy and space exploration. A small planetarium is available by arrangement. School parties must book at the observatory, but details of other educational services can be obtained from McManus Galleries.

ROYAL RESEARCH SHIP 'DISCOVERY'

Dundee Industrial Heritage Ltd., 26 East Dock Street, Dundee DD1 9HY
Tel:(0382) 201175

Cutty Sark Maritime Trust

Open Apr-7 Oct Mon-Fri 1-5 Sat-Sun 11-5.
Admission charges (with concessions)
P, R/ST, <50%, WC, G

Victoria Dock, near town centre, parking for cars & coaches, sales area, wc, parties welcome but must book.

Royal Research Ship 'Discovery' was used by Captain Robert Falcon Scott on the National Antarctic Expedition of 1901-1904. Since being returned to Dundee where she was built, the ship is being completely refurbished. Visitors are guided around the ship in small groups which leave at regular intervals.

ST MARY'S TOWER (OLD STEEPLE)

Kirk Style, Nethergate, Dundee
Correspondence to McManus Galleries, Albert Square, Dundee DD1 1DA. Tel:(0382) 23141.

City of Dundee District Council

Open by appointment. Admission free.

City centre, parties welcome but must book.

A 15th century tower restored by Gilbert Scott in the 19th century with many historic associations and a wonderful view over the city centre.

DUNKELD

DUNKELD CATHEDRAL CHAPTER HOUSE MUSEUM

Dunkeld, Perthshire
Tel:(035 02) 249

The Kirk Session of Dunkeld

Open Easter-Remembrance Sun (early Nov) daily 9.30-7. Admission free.
P, L, 50%, H, G

Town centre 1/4 mile off A9, parking for cars & coaches, parties welcome no need to book.

A small collection of graphic/documentary material and objects relating to the cathedral and the Atholl district.

THE SCOTTISH HORSE MUSEUM

The Cross, Dunkeld, Perthshire

The Scottish Horse Trustees

Open Easter, Whitsun-Sep daily 10-12 & 2-5. Admission charges.

Town centre 1/4 mile off A9, parking for cars & coaches, parties welcome no need to book.

The only independent Highland Yeomanry Regimental Museum in the country contains varied displays telling the history of the Scottish Horse Yeomanry, from its raising in Scotland and South Africa in 1900 to its amalgamation with the Fife & Forfar Yeomanry in 1956.

ERROL

ERROL STATION RAILWAY HERITAGE CENTRE

Errol Station, Errol, Perthshire
Tel:(05754) 222

Errol Station Trust

Open May-Sep Sat-Sun 10-4. Admission charges.
P, L, 50%, WC, G, C, B, AD

1/2 mile off A85 Dundee-Perth road, parking for cars & coaches, refreshments, sales area, wc.

This museum, opening in 1990, is housed in the 1847 Errol Station, a fine example of a Scottish country railway station on the main Aberdeen-Glasgow line. The former porter's house now displays a collection of items relating to the history of the rural railways in Tayside. The booking office, general waiting room and ladies' waiting room have been restored to their 1920's appearance, and house photographs, documents and objects relating to Dundee and Perth railway history.

GLAMIS

ANGUS FOLK MUSEUM

Kirkwynd Cottages, Glamis, Angus
Tel:(030 784) 288

National Trust for Scotland

Open mid Apr-Sep daily 11-5. Last admission 4.30. Admission charges (with concessions).
P, L, <50%, G, AD

Glamis 12 miles north of Dundee off A94, parking nearby, parties welcome but must book.

Folklore specialist and casual visitor alike will enjoy a visit to this museum with its displays of domestic and farm implements, photographs and archives.

GLAMIS CASTLE

Glamis, Angus DD8 1RJ
Tel:(030 784) 242

Strathmore Estates (Holding) Ltd.

Open daily mid Apr-mid Oct 12-5.30 (last tour 4.45). Admission charges (with concessions).
P, R, ST, WC, G, C

5 miles west of Forfar on A94, parking for cars & coaches, refreshments, sales area, temporary exhibitions, wc, parties welcome no need to book.

Glamis Castle is the family home of the Earls of Strathmore and Kinghorne. It is the childhood home of HM Queen Elizabeth the Queen Mother, birthplace of HRH The Princess Margaret and the legendary setting of Shakespeare's play 'Macbeth'. The Castle is a five-storey 'L' shaped tower block dating from the 14th century. It was remodelled in the 17th century and contains magnificent rooms with a wide range of historic pictures, furniture, porcelain and tapestries.

KINNESSWOOD

MICHAEL BRUCE COTTAGE MUSEUM

The Cobbles, Kinnesswood, Kinross
Contact Dr D M Munro Tel:(031) 556 0307.

Michael Bruce Memorial Trust

Open Apr-Sep daily 9-5. Keys from The Garage, Kinnesswood. Admission free.
PPA, ST, 50%

4 miles east of Kinross, sales area, parties welcome but must book.

A cottage which was the home of Michael Bruce, the 'Gentle Poet of Loch Leven' who died in 1767 at the age of 21. There is a collection of items from Scottish village life in the 18th and 19th centuries.

KINROSS

KINROSS MUSEUM

High Street, Kinross, Perthshire
Correspondence to Curator, Perth Museum & Art Gallery, George Street, Perth. Tel:(0738) 32488.

Perth & Kinross District Council

Open May-Sep Tue-Sat 1-5. Admission free.
ST, G

Centre of Kinross off M90, parties welcome but must book.

A small museum with some interesting items relating to the social history of Kinross and the surrounding countryside.

KIRRIEMUIR

BARRIE'S BIRTHPLACE

9 Brechin Road, Kirriemuir, Angus DD8 4BX
Tel:(0575) 72646

National Trust for Scotland

Open Easter & May-Sep Mon-Sat 11-5.30 Sun 2-5.30. Last admission 1/2 hour before closing. Admission charges (with concessions).
P, ST, <50%, G

6 miles north west of Forfar on A926, parking for cars & coaches, parties welcome but must book as limited space.

Whether or not you have ever grown up, you will enjoy the birthplace of Peter Pan's creator. The museum contains J.M. Barrie's works, many of his personal possessions, two early Peter Pan costumes and his first theatre in the wash-house.

MEIGLE

MEIGLE MUSEUM

Meigle, Perthshire
Tel:(031) 244 3101 for information.

Scottish Development Department (Historic Buildings and Monuments)

Open Jan-Mar & Oct-Dec Mon-Sat 9.30-4 Apr-Sep Mon-Sat 9.30-7. Admission charges (with concessions).
L, G

Town centre.

A stunning collection of sculptured monuments of the Celtic Church period, all found nearby, are housed in this old school. The whole collection forms one of the most notable assemblages of Dark Age sculpture in Western Europe.

MONTROSE

HOUSE OF DUN

Montrose, Angus DD10 9LQ.
Tel:(067 481) 238

National Trust for Scotland

Open Easter, May-Oct daily 11-5.30. Admission charges (with concessions).
PPA, ST, <50%, WC, G, C

4 miles west of Montrose on A935, parking for cars & coaches, refreshments, wc, parties welcome but must book.

Palladian house overlooking the Montrose Basin, built in 1730 for David Erskine, Lord Dun, to designs by William Adam. The house has been restored by the Trust, including the exuberant plasterwork in the saloon, originally by Joseph Enser. A special exhibition on the architecture of the house is on display.

MONTROSE MUSEUM & ART GALLERY

Panmure Place, Montrose DD10 8HE
Tel:(0674) 73232

Angus District Council

Open Apr-Oct Mon-Sat 10.30-1 & 2-5 Jul-Aug also open Sun 2-5 Nov-Mar Mon-Fri 2-5 Sat 10.30-1 & 2-5. Admission free.
PPA, ST, 50%, G

Town centre, parking for cars, coaches must book, sales area, wc, parties welcome but must book.

A district history museum with extensive local collections which include three Pictish stones, the sword of the Marquis of Montrose, Montrose silver and pottery and the Lord Gray agate collection. The maritime gallery has early whaling artefacts and a small collection of Napoleonic items including a cast of Napoleon's death mask. The art gallery has a collection of paintings by local artists and local views and includes sculptures by William Lamb and paintings by George Paul Chalmers.

SUNNYSIDE ROYAL HOSPITAL MUSEUM

Montrose DD10 9JP
Tel:(067 483) 361

Tayside Health Board

Open Easter-end Nov Wed 2-3.30. Admission free.
P, L, 100%, G, C

2 1/2 miles north of Montrose off A937, parking for cars, refreshments, sales area, wc, parties welcome but must book.

Situated in a psychiatric hospital, this unusual museum illustrates the history of psychiatry in Scotland and Sunnyside Royal Hospital.

WILLIAM LAMB MEMORIAL STUDIO

24 Market Street, Montrose
Correspondence to Montrose Museum & Art Gallery, Panmure Place, Montrose DD10 8HE. Tel:(0674) 73232.

Angus District Council

Open Jul & Aug Sun only 2-5. Other times by appointment. Admission free.
PPA, L, 50%, G

In town, sales area, wc, parties welcome but must book.

Memorial gallery to William Lamb A.R.S.A (1893-1951) showing his sculpture studio, workshop and living room set out with a selection of the artist's works (sculptures, wood carvings, etchings, drawings, watercolours) along with modelling and woodcarving tools and Lamb's original furniture.

PERTH

THE BLACK WATCH MUSEUM

Balhousie Castle, Hay Street, Perth PH1 5HR
Tel:(0738) 21281 ex 8530

The Black Watch Regimental Trust

Open all year Mon-Fri 10-4.30 (winter 3.30) also Easter-Sep Sun & public holidays 2-4.30. Other times by appointment. Admission free.
PPA, L, <50%, G

1 mile north of city centre beside North Inch, parking nearby, sales area, wc, parties welcome but must book.

A fascinating array of pictures, medals, uniforms and other military relics telling the story of the Black Watch Royal Highland Regiment from its founding in 1739 to the present day.

PERTH MUSEUM & ART GALLERY

George Street, Perth PH1 5LB
Tel:(0738) 32488

Perth & Kinross District Council

Open all year Mon-Sat 10-5. Admission free.
P, ST, 50%, WC, G

Town centre, parking nearby, temporary exhibitions, wc, parties welcome (must book for talks/guide).

This purpose-built museum holds important collections of fine art (including Scottish painting), applied art (Perth silver and glass), archaeology and natural history. It also has notable collections of ethnography.

SCONE PALACE

Perth PH2 6BD
Tel:(0738) 52300

Earl of Mansfield

Open Easter-mid Oct Mon-Sat 9.30-5 Sun 1.30-5, Jul-Aug also Sun 10-5. Other times by appointment. Admission charges (with concessions).
ST, 100%, WC, G, C, B

2 miles from Perth on A93, parking for cars & coaches, refreshments sales area, temporary exhibitions, wc, parties welcome but must book.

A crowning place of Scottish kings including Macbeth and Robert the Bruce, Scone Palace has treasures of porcelain, 17th and 18th century ivories, antique furniture and needlework, including bed hangings worked by Mary Queen of Scots. A permanent exhibition on estate management, a display of agricultural implements and a living collection of rare conifers are among other attractions. Special rates and facilities for school parties.

WEEM

CASTLE MENZIES

Weem, by Aberfeldy, Perthshire
Tel:(0887) 20982

The Menzies Clan Society

Open Apr-Oct Mon-Sat 10.30-5 Sun 2-5. Admission charges (with concessions).
P, L/ST, <50%, G

1/2 mile west of Weem on B846, parking for cars & coaches, sales area, temporary exhibitions, wc, parties welcome but must book.

This 16th century castle undergoing restoration contains a small but interesting collection of artefacts associated with Clan Menzies.

Western Isles

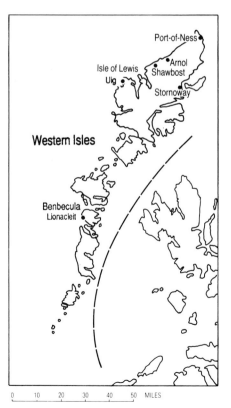

Western Isles

Port-of-Ness

Isle of Lewis
Uig
Arnol
Shawbost
Stornoway

Benbecula
Lionacleit

0   10   20   30   40   50   MILES

BLACK HOUSE

Arnol, Isle of Lewis
Tel:(031) 556 8400 for information.

Scottish Development Department (Historic Buildings and Monuments)

Open Apr-Sep Mon-Sat 9.30-7 Sun 2-7 Oct-Mar Sat 9.30-4 Sun 2-4. Admission charges.

Centre of village.

A good example of a traditional type of Hebridean dwelling, appropriately furnished.

MUSEUM NAN EILEAN

Sgoil Lionacleit, Lionacleit, Island of Benbecula
Tel:(0870) 2211

Comhairle Nan Eileen/Western Isles Islands Council

Open all year Mon,Wed,Thu 9-4 Tue,Fri 9-8, Sat 11-4. Admission free.
PPA, L/R, 100%, WC, G, C

Parking for cars & coaches, temporary exhibitions, wc, parties welcome.

This museum is located within a recently opened community school. It operates a varied annual programme of exhibitions on a wide range of themes. Audio-visual and photographic material on aspects of the history and culture of the Islands is available for consultation.

NESS

COMUNN EACHDRAIDH NIS/ NESS HISTORICAL SOCIETY

Lionel Old School and Dell Mill, Port-of-Ness, Isle of Lewis PA86 0TA
Tel:(085 181) 576

Comunn Eachdraidh Nis / Ness Historical Society

Open Jun-Sep Mon-Fri 9-5. Admission free.
P, 50%, WC

28 miles north of Stornoway, parking for cars & coaches, sales area, wc, parties welcome no need to book.

A collection of artefacts relating to crofting and past domestic life in the district of Ness, with documentary and audio-visual archives. Dell Mill is a recently restored 19th century grain mill with a full range of equipment and machinery together with interpretive displays on the mill and local grain production.

SHAWBOST

SHAWBOST SCHOOL

Shawbost, Isle of Lewis
Tel:(085) 171 213

Shawbost School

Open Apr-Oct Mon-Sat 10-6. Admission free.
P, L, 50%, G

West coast of Lewis, parking for cars & coaches, wc, parties welcome no need to book.

Local schoolchildren have put together this permanent exhibition of objects relating to crofting, fishing and domestic life in Lewis. Statistics compiled by the children show the changing patterns of life on the island.

STORNOWAY

AN LANNTAIR

Stornoway Town Hall, Stornoway, Isle of Lewis PA87 2BE
Tel:(0851) 3307

An Lanntair Ltd.

Open all year Mon-Sat 10-5.30. Admission free.
ST, 100%, G

Town centre, parking nearby, temporary exhibitions, wc, parties welcome no need to book.

An Lanntair is situated upstairs in Stornoway Town Hall with a commanding view of the harbour. Exhibitions change every month, with an emphasis on local artists' work during the summer months and on touring exhibitions during the winter. The gallery also operates a diverse events programme of music, readings, performance etc. An Lanntair has a firm commitment to the Gaelic language and actively promotes traditional Gaelic arts.

MUSEUM NAN EILEAN

Sandwick Road, Town Hall, Stornoway, Isle of Lewis PA87 2BW
Tel:(0851) 3773 ex.305

Comhairle Nan Eileen/Western Isles Islands Council

Open all year Jun-Aug Tue-Sat 10-12 & 2-5.30 Sep-May Tue-Sat 2-5. Admission free.
L, 50%, G

Town centre, parking for cars & coaches, temporary exhibitions, wc, parties welcome but must book.

The museum contains displays of objects and photographs illustrating aspects of the history of Lewis and the town of Stornoway. Sections are devoted to fishing and maritime history, domestic life, agriculture and archaeology.

UIG

COMUNN EACHDRAIDH UIG/ UIG HISTORICAL SOCIETY

Loch Croistean Centre, Uig, Isle of Lewis

Comunn Eachdraidh Uig / Uig Historical Society

Open Jul-Aug Mon-Sat 11-6. Admission charges.
P, WC

Parking for cars & coaches, wc, parties welcome.

The centre contains an exhibition on crofting life in the area, featuring photographs, artefacts and documentary material with detailed histories of the crofting villages and crofting families of the area.

Index